AI Unleashed: Prompt Engineering and Development for Business Transformation

Dan Pearson

Published by Dan Pearson, 2023.

AI UNLEASHED: PROMPT ENGINEERING AND DEVELOPMENT FOR BUSINESS TRANSFORMATION

First edition. May 16, 2023.

ISBN: 979-8988409328

Written by Dan Pearson.

AI Unleashed: Prompt Engineering and Development for Business Transformation

Prologue

As we enter the fourth industrial revolution, the transformative power of Artificial Intelligence (AI) is unmistakable. It's changing every aspect of our lives, from work and communication to business and resource management, heralding a shift unlike any before.

"The AI Frontier: Unleashing the Power of Artificial Intelligence in Business" is more than a guide—it's a journey that challenges the conventional limits of business literature. This book explores AI's rise, current applications, future business possibilities, and ethical considerations. It goes beyond understanding AI, stimulating critical thinking about AI's potential and ethical implications in business.

In the following chapters, we'll explore AI's role in decision-making, customer engagement, and business model innovation. We'll tackle the challenges of AI implementation and offer insights on overcoming them.

AI isn't just a tool—it's an opportunity, a frontier to be explored, capable of redefining business operations and opening new pathways for efficiency and growth. But these opportunities also bring challenges—ethical, operational, and societal. Navigating these challenges is crucial to fully leverage AI's power.

"The AI Frontier" aims to equip business leaders with the knowledge to confidently guide their organizations into an AI-driven future. It blends research-based insights with real-world case studies and practical advice, making it a comprehensive resource for anyone interested in AI's intersection with business.

As we traverse the AI frontier, our goal is to understand, adapt, and integrate—not conquer or control. We're not just exploring technology; we're exploring a new business mindset for an increasingly interconnected and intelligent world.

Chapter 1

Understanding AI: From Basics to Business

A

s we embark on this remarkable expedition to explore the game-changing potential of Artificial Intelligence (AI) in the business realm, it is imperative to commence with a solid comprehension of AI itself. This initial chapter serves as a comprehensive introduction to AI, laying the groundwork for the rest of the book.

We commence by elucidating the concept of AI, delving into its various aspects, and demystifying the technical terminology associated with it. From machine learning to deep learning, neural networks to natural language processing, we will break down these intricate terms and concepts into easily digestible morsels, ensuring a clear understanding of the technology that is reshaping the business landscape.

Subsequently, we trace the evolution of AI, from its conceptualization in the mid-20th century to its current standing as one of the most influential technologies of our time. This historical perspective will enable us to truly appreciate the transformative power of AI and its potential to revolutionize business processes and models.

Lastly, we provide an overview of AI in the business domain. From automating mundane tasks to facilitating strategic decision-making, from personalizing customer experiences to fostering innovation in products and services, we will explore the myriad ways in which AI is being harnessed in the business arena.

This chapter establishes the foundation for a more profound exploration of AI's role and potential in business, which will be further explored in subsequent chapters. By the conclusion of this chapter, you will have a comprehensive understanding of what AI entails, its evolution, and the potential impact it holds for the business landscape.

So, let us embark on this enlightening journey of unraveling AI: from fundamentals to business.

What is AI?

Artificial Intelligence (AI) is a term that frequently arises in conversations about technology and the future. But what does it truly encompass? In its simplest form, AI represents a branch of computer science dedicated to creating and implementing machines capable of executing tasks that typically necessitate human intelligence. These tasks encompass comprehending natural language, identifying patterns, learning from experience, drawing conclusions, and making predictions or decisions.

While this definition provides a basic understanding of AI, it is essential to delve deeper into the distinct types of AI and their capabilities.

Types of AI

AI can be broadly categorized into two types: Narrow AI and General AI.

Narrow AI, also known as Weak AI, is the type of AI that we interact with in our daily lives. It is designed to perform a specific task, such as voice recognition, recommendation systems, or image recognition. It operates under a limited set of constraints and is 'trained' to do a specific task. Examples include Siri, Amazon's Alexa, or a chatbot on a website. While these systems may seem intelligent and can make tasks more efficient, they operate under a narrowly defined range of functions and don't possess the ability to understand, learn, or apply knowledge outside of their specific programmed function.

On the other hand, General AI, also known as Strong AI, refers to systems that possess the ability to understand, learn, adapt, and implement knowledge across a wide range of tasks. These systems can independently apply intelligence to different problems and adapt to new situations. They would have a consciousness, sentience, and mind of their own, similar to human intelligence. As of now, General AI remains largely theoretical, with no practical examples in use today.

Components of AI

AI encompasses a wide range of technologies, including Machine Learning (ML), Deep Learning (DL), Natural Language Processing (NLP), and Robotics.

Machine Learning is a subset of AI that provides systems the ability to learn from data and improve from experience without being explicitly programmed. It uses statistical techniques to enable machines to improve at tasks with experience. It is the ML that is behind the recommendation systems of Netflix and Amazon, the voice recognition of Siri and Alexa, and the search algorithms of Google.

Deep Learning, a further subset of machine learning, is inspired by the structure of the human brain and creates an artificial neural network that can learn and make intelligent decisions on its own. Deep learning is particularly effective when it comes to processing large volumes of data, making it extremely valuable for tasks like image and speech recognition.

Natural Language Processing involves the interaction between computers and human language. It allows machines to understand, interpret, generate, and respond to human language in a valuable way. This technology is widely used in applications such as automated customer service, language translation apps, and voice-activated assistants.

Robotics is a field that intersects with AI, where programmed entities are used to perform tasks that are dangerous, tedious, or repetitive. When combined with AI, robotics can provide machines with the ability to perceive, understand, navigate, and manipulate the physical world.

The Power of AI

The power of AI lies in its ability to learn, adapt, and process information at a scale and speed far beyond human capability. It has the potential to transform a wide range of industries, from healthcare and education to finance, transportation, and entertainment. By automating routine tasks, AI can increase efficiency and productivity. By providing deep insights and predictive analytics, it can aid in decision-making and strategic planning. By personalizing interactions and services it can enhance user experience and customer satisfaction. And by innovating new products and services, it can drive growth and competitiveness.

AI is not without its challenges, however. Issues around data privacy, security, ethical use of AI, and the impact on employment are significant concerns that need to be addressed. Moreover, the successful implementation of AI requires a solid data infrastructure, skilled talent, and a strategic approach. Despite these challenges, the potential benefits of AI make it a technology worth investing in.

Conclusion

Understanding AI is not just about understanding a technology; it's about understanding a transformative force that is reshaping our world. From its definition to its types, components, and potential impact, a clear grasp of AI is essential for anyone looking to navigate the AI frontier.

However, it's important to note that AI is a rapidly evolving field, and what we know today may be surpassed by new developments tomorrow. Thus, staying updated with the latest advancements is as crucial as understanding the basics.

As we move forward in this book, we'll delve deeper into the various applications of AI in business, explore how businesses can build an AI-ready organization and strategy, and examine the challenges and ethical considerations associated with AI.

By understanding AI, we take the first step towards harnessing its power. As the saying goes, knowledge is power. In the context of AI, knowledge is not just power; it's a pathway to transformation and growth.

In the next section, we will trace the evolution of AI, from its inception to its current state, providing a historical context to the development of this groundbreaking technology. Through this exploration, we aim to enhance your understanding of AI, setting the stage for a deeper dive into its applications and implications in the business world.

The Evolution of AI

The story of Artificial Intelligence (AI) is a captivating odyssey, spanning several decades of relentless research, groundbreaking innovation, and continuous evolution. To truly grasp AI's current state and envision its future trajectory, it is imperative to delve into its intriguing history.

The Birth of an Idea

The origins of AI can be traced back to antiquity, where ancient myths and tales showcased artificial beings endowed with intellect and consciousness by masterful craftsmen. Nonetheless, the scientific pursuit of AI, as we comprehend it today, embarked on its earnest journey in the mid-20th century. The term "Artificial Intelligence" was ingeniously coined by John McCarthy in 1956 during the illustrious Dartmouth conference, laying the foundation for AI as a distinguished field of scientific inquiry.

Early AI Research: 1950s to 1970s

The nascent years of AI research were brimming with boundless optimism. Pioneering researchers dared to envision a future where machines would possess intelligence akin to humans within a few short decades. It was during this period that the first AI programs came to life, astounding the world with their ingenuity. Among these remarkable programs was the Logic Theorist, masterfully crafted by Allen Newell and Herbert A. Simon, often hailed as the progenitor of AI programs. Equally impressive was ELIZA, the brainchild of Joseph Weizenbaum at MIT, which skillfully simulated a psychotherapist by ingeniously rephrasing patient statements as probing questions.

AI Winter: Late 1970s to Late 1980s

Despite the early euphoria surrounding AI, progress proved to be more arduous than anticipated. The sheer complexity of real-world problems posed formidable challenges to the comparatively rudimentary AI systems of that era. Consequently, funding for AI research dwindled, plunging the field into what became known as the "AI winter." Nevertheless, even amidst this chilling period, valuable work continued to persevere. Expert systems, designed to emulate the decision-making prowess of human experts, gained popularity, while fundamental advancements in machine learning laid sturdy groundwork for future breakthroughs.

AI Renaissance: Late 1980s to Early 2000s

The late 1980s witnessed a renaissance in AI as faster computers and an abundance of data reignited the spark of interest in this captivating field. The development of algorithms capable of handling vast datasets led to significant strides in machine learning. AI began to seamlessly integrate into everyday technologies, be it recommendation systems that fine-tuned personalized experiences or speech recognition that breathed life into our interactions with machines.

The Era of Big Data and Deep Learning: 2010s Onwards

The 2010s emerged as a pivotal juncture in AI's saga. The advent of big data, coupled with extraordinary advancements in computing power and storage capabilities, set the stage for the ascendance of deep learning. These formidable algorithms, endowed with the ability to learn from copious amounts of data, quickly outshone their counterparts, revolutionizing various domains. From the mesmerizing realms of computer vision to the intricate nuances of natural language processing, breakthroughs became the norm.

AI systems, once considered novelties, grew increasingly proficient, effortlessly tackling tasks that were once thought to be exclusive to the realm of human cognition. In a stunning display of prowess, IBM's Watson triumphed over human champions in a game of Jeopardy in 2011, while Google's AlphaGo astounded the world by defeating a world champion at the game of Go, widely regarded as a profound test of intellect.

The Current State of AI

In the present day, AI has permeated every facet of our lives, solidifying its position as a formidable force and a focal point of research and development. Its applications are ubiquitous, ranging from the familiar voice assistants like Siri and Alexa, to the sophisticated recommendation systems employed by industry giants such as Amazon and Netflix. AI's reach extends to transformative technologies like self-driving cars and AI-powered healthcare diagnostics, where it demonstrates its potential to revolutionize entire industries.

The Future of AI

As we gaze into the future, the prospects for AI appear boundless. Advances in AI are poised to catalyze profound transformations across various sectors. The potential applications of AI are vast and diverse, from personalized education that caters to individual needs, to the creation of smarter cities that enhance sustainability. The impact of AI on healthcare holds immense promise, enabling improved diagnostics, precision medicine, and enhanced patient care. Furthermore, AI is expected to drive substantial economic growth and usher in unprecedented productivity improvements.

However, the path towards an AI-powered future is not devoid of challenges. Critical issues such as data privacy and security, ethical considerations surrounding the use of AI, and the potential impact on employment require careful attention and deliberation. Moreover, as AI systems grow increasingly complex and powerful, new questions and challenges are likely to arise, necessitating ongoing research and responsible development.

The future of AI is intrinsically linked to advancements in related fields such as big data, computing power, and machine learning algorithms. These interconnected disciplines continuously push the boundaries of what AI can achieve, unlocking new possibilities and driving innovation.

Conclusion

The history of AI is a testament to human ingenuity and persistence. From its conceptual origins to its current state, the journey of AI has been marked by grand visions, hard-learned lessons, and remarkable advancements.

As we delve deeper into AI's role and potential in business, this historical perspective will serve as a valuable backdrop. By understanding the evolution of AI, we can better appreciate its potential and prepare for its future.

In the next section, we will explore the role of AI in business. We will examine how AI is transforming business processes, enabling new business models, and driving strategic decision-making. Through this exploration, we aim to equip you with the knowledge and insights to harness the power of AI in your business journey.

AI in Business: An Overview

As we've explored in the previous sections, Artificial Intelligence (AI) is a rapidly evolving field with transformative potential. One of the areas where this potential is most evident is in the world of business. From automating routine tasks to making strategic decisions, AI is changing the way businesses operate and compete.

Transforming Business Processes

As we have explored in previous sections, Artificial Intelligence (AI) is a rapidly evolving field with transformative potential. Nowhere is this potential more evident than in the realm of business. AI is revolutionizing the way businesses operate and compete, from automating routine tasks to enabling strategic decision-making.

At the operational level, AI offers the power to automate mundane and repetitive tasks, thereby increasing efficiency and freeing up human workers to focus on more complex and creative endeavors.

Organizations are employing AI-powered automation in various applications, ranging from customer service chatbots that provide instant support to intelligent document analysis systems that streamline data entry processes.

Furthermore, AI is enhancing business processes by providing valuable insights that help companies optimize their operations. By analyzing vast amounts of operational data, AI can identify bottlenecks, inefficiencies, and opportunities for improvement. These insights enable organizations to make data-driven decisions and optimize their processes for greater productivity and cost-effectiveness.

Driving Strategic Decision-Making

AI is also playing a pivotal role in strategic decision-making for businesses. With its capacity to analyze large datasets and uncover patterns, AI empowers organizations with deep insights that inform crucial strategic decisions.

For instance, AI can analyze market trends, consumer behavior, and competitive dynamics to provide valuable inputs for decisions regarding product development, pricing strategies, and market entry. By leveraging AI's analytical capabilities, businesses can gain a comprehensive understanding of their target markets and make informed choices that drive their competitive advantage.

Moreover, AI's predictive capabilities enable businesses to anticipate future trends and scenarios, facilitating proactive decision-making. By leveraging historical data and advanced algorithms, AI can generate forecasts and projections, helping organizations plan and adapt to potential challenges or opportunities.

Enabling New Business Models

In addition to enhancing existing business processes and decision-making, AI is enabling the emergence of entirely new business models that were previously unattainable.

For example, AI lies at the core of recommendation systems used by companies like Amazon and Netflix. These systems analyze user behavior, preferences, and historical data to provide personalized recommendations, thereby driving customer engagement and sales. The ability to personalize at scale, made possible by AI, has revolutionized the way businesses interact with their customers.

Similarly, AI is enabling business models centered around predictive maintenance in industries such as manufacturing and aviation. By leveraging AI algorithms that analyze equipment data, businesses can predict maintenance needs and detect potential failures in advance. This proactive approach reduces downtime, optimizes maintenance schedules, and minimizes costs associated with unexpected breakdowns.

Challenges in Implementing AI in Business

While the potential of AI in business is immense, its implementation is not without challenges. Organizations must address various technical, organizational, and ethical considerations.

Technical challenges include the need for large volumes of high-quality data to train AI models effectively. Additionally, AI systems can be complex and require skilled expertise in areas such as machine learning and data science.

Organizational challenges involve integrating AI into existing processes and systems. This requires collaboration between different departments, ensuring data interoperability, and upskilling employees to work effectively with AI technologies.

Ethical and regulatory challenges are also pertinent. Businesses must navigate issues related to data privacy, ensuring that customer information is handled responsibly and in compliance with regulations. Furthermore, concerns regarding algorithmic bias and the impact of AI on employment need to be addressed to ensure fairness and inclusivity.

Despite these challenges, businesses that successfully implement AI stand to gain a competitive edge, enhanced efficiency, and the ability to drive innovation. As AI continues to evolve, organizations must embrace its transformative potential while proactively addressing the challenges to unlock its full benefits.

Conclusion

AI is transforming the world of business, driving efficiency, insight, and innovation. To harness the power of AI, businesses need to understand not only the technology itself but also how it can be applied to create value in their specific context.

In the coming sections, we will delve deeper into the applications of AI in different business functions, explore how businesses can build an AI-ready organization and strategy, and examine the ethical and regulatory considerations in implementing AI.

By understanding AI in business, we equip ourselves to navigate the AI frontier in business, leveraging AI's potential to drive growth and competitiveness.

In the next section, we will explore AI's role in customer relationship management, a key business function where AI's impact is already visible and transformative.

Chapter 2

AI in Decision-Making

I

n an increasingly complex and data-driven world, making informed decisions quickly and accurately is crucial for the success of any business. This is where Artificial Intelligence (AI) comes into play. AI, with its ability to process vast amounts of data and uncover insights, is revolutionizing the process of decision-making in business.

In this chapter, we will delve into the role of AI in decision-making. We will explore how AI is transforming strategic and operational decisions, the different AI tools and technologies that support decision-making, and the implications of AI-powered decisions for businesses.

We will begin by discussing the traditional decision-making process and its limitations in the modern business environment. From there, we will explore how AI overcomes these limitations by providing data-driven insights, predictive analytics, and real-time decision support.

Next, we will examine the different AI technologies that facilitate decision-making. This will include an overview of machine learning, data mining, predictive modeling, and decision support systems. We will also discuss the role of big data in AI-powered decision-making, and how businesses can leverage it effectively.

In the subsequent sections, we will look at the practical applications of AI in decision-making across different business functions – from marketing and sales to supply chain management and human resources. We will share real-world case studies that illustrate the transformative impact of AI in these areas.

Finally, we will discuss the ethical and societal implications of AI in decision-making. While AI offers significant advantages in terms of efficiency and accuracy, it also raises important questions about data privacy, algorithmic bias, and the role of human judgment in decision-making. We will explore these issues in depth and discuss the best practices for ethical and responsible use of AI in decision-making.

By the end of this chapter, you will have a deep understanding of the role and potential of AI in decision-making. You will also be equipped with the knowledge to evaluate the opportunities and challenges presented by AI in your own decision-making processes.

Let's embark on this journey to explore how AI is reshaping the landscape of decision-making in the world of business.

The Role of AI in Business Decisions

Artificial Intelligence (AI) is transforming the landscape of decision-making in business. By analyzing vast amounts of data and learning from this data, AI is providing businesses with unprecedented levels of insight and predictive power, fundamentally changing how they make decisions.

Overcoming Limitations of Traditional Decision-Making

In the traditional decision-making process, businesses often rely on human experience and intuition. However, this approach has several limitations. First, humans can only process a limited amount of information at a time, making it difficult to handle the vast amounts of data available today. Second, human decision-making is often biased and prone to errors. Third, humans may struggle to keep up with the rapid pace of change in today's business environment.

AI overcomes these limitations. It can process and analyze vast amounts of data far beyond human capacity, uncovering patterns and insights that humans would likely miss. It can also make unbiased decisions based on data, reducing errors. Furthermore, AI can adapt to changes in the environment quickly and efficiently, making it well-suited for today's dynamic business world.

Data-Driven Insights

One of the key ways in which AI transforms decision-making is by providing data-driven insights. With the ability to process and analyze large datasets, AI can uncover patterns and correlations that are not immediately apparent to the human eye. These insights can inform a wide range of business decisions, from identifying new market opportunities to improving operational efficiency.

For example, a retail company could use AI to analyze customer data and identify buying patterns. This could inform decisions about product placement, marketing strategies, and even product development. Similarly, a manufacturing company could use AI to analyze operational data and identify inefficiencies, informing decisions about process improvement and resource allocation.

Predictive Analytics

In addition to providing insights based on past and present data, AI can also predict future outcomes. This is known as predictive analytics. By analyzing historical data and identifying trends, AI can forecast future events with a high degree of accuracy.

For instance, a financial services company could use AI to predict market trends and inform investment decisions. Similarly, a healthcare provider could use AI to predict patient outcomes and inform treatment decisions. By providing a glimpse into the future, AI empowers businesses to make proactive decisions and stay ahead of the curve.

Real-Time Decision Support

AI also provides real-time decision support. With the ability to process and analyze data in real-time, AI can provide businesses with timely and relevant insights, enabling them to make quick and informed decisions.

For example, an e-commerce company could use AI to analyze real-time customer behavior data and make immediate decisions about product recommendations or personalized offers. Similarly, a logistics company could use AI to analyze real-time traffic and weather data and make instant decisions about route optimization.

Challenges and Considerations

While AI offers significant benefits for decision-making, it also presents several challenges. These include the need for high-quality data, the complexity of AI models, and the risk of over-reliance on AI at the expense of human judgment.

In addition, businesses must consider ethical and regulatory issues related to AI, such as data privacy, algorithmic bias, and transparency in decision-making. It's important for businesses to navigate these challenges effectively to harness the full potential of AI in decision-making.

Conclusion

AI is transforming decision-making in business, providing data-driven insights, predictive analytics, and real-time decision support. By overcoming the limitations of traditional decision-making, AI empowers businesses to make more informed, accurate, and proactive decisions. However, to harness the full potential of AI in decision-making, businesses must effectively navigate the challenges and considerations associated with AI.

As we delve deeper into this chapter, we will explore the different AI technologies that facilitate decision-making, discuss the role of big data in AI-powered decision-making, and examine the practical applications of AI in decision-making across different business functions.

In the next section, we'll take a closer look at machine learning, a key AI technology that powers data-driven decision-making. We'll discuss how machine learning works, the different types of machine learning, and how businesses can use machine learning to inform their decisions.

Whether you are a business leader seeking to understand how AI can improve your decision-making process, or a professional looking to leverage AI in your role, this exploration of AI's role in business decisions aims to provide you with a clear and comprehensive understanding.

The future of decision-making in business is being shaped by AI. By understanding and embracing this transformation, businesses can unlock new levels of efficiency, accuracy, and strategic insight in their decision-making processes. The revolution is here, and it's time for businesses to step into the new world of AI-powered decision-making.

Case Studies: AI in Decision-Making

Artificial Intelligence (AI) is no longer a futuristic concept; it's a present reality transforming the way businesses operate and make decisions. To understand the practical implications of AI in decision-making, let's explore some real-world case studies from different industry sectors.

Retail: Optimizing Inventory with AI

One of the significant challenges in the retail industry is inventory management. Predicting the right amount of stock to keep on hand is a complex task, especially considering factors like seasonal trends, customer behavior, and supply chain disruptions.

Walmart, the world's largest retailer, turned to AI to tackle this challenge. They developed an AI-powered demand forecasting model that analyzes historical sales data, promotional information, and external factors like weather and holidays to predict future demand for different products. This predictive power has enabled Walmart to optimize their inventory, reducing overstock and stockouts, and ultimately improving customer satisfaction.

Healthcare: Predicting Patient Outcomes with AI

AI is making significant strides in healthcare, particularly in predicting patient outcomes. The Mayo Clinic, a leading healthcare organization, uses AI to predict which patients are likely to have complications or readmissions. By analyzing electronic health record (EHR) data, the AI model identifies patients at risk and allows healthcare providers to intervene proactively. This early intervention leads to improved patient care and reduced healthcare costs.

Finance: Enhancing Risk Assessment with AI

Financial institutions have been early adopters of AI in decision-making, particularly in the realm of risk assessment. JP Morgan Chase uses AI to assess credit risk, which is the likelihood that a borrower will default on a loan. The AI model analyzes a vast array of data, including the borrower's financial history, macroeconomic indicators, and even social media activity, to predict credit risk. This AI-powered risk assessment has improved the accuracy of credit decisions, reducing losses for the bank.

Manufacturing: Improving Quality Control with AI

In the manufacturing sector, quality control is a critical area where AI is making a difference. General Electric (GE) uses AI-powered image recognition technology to inspect its products for defects. The AI model is trained to recognize various defect types using thousands of images. Once trained, the model can inspect products in real-time, identifying defects more accurately and faster than human inspectors. This AI application has led to significant improvements in product quality and manufacturing efficiency.

Transportation: Optimizing Routes with AI

In the transportation industry, optimizing routes is a key decision-making area where AI is having an impact. UPS, a global logistics company, uses AI to determine the most efficient delivery routes for its drivers. The AI-powered system, known as ORION (On-Road Integrated Optimization and Navigation), analyzes factors like traffic, weather, and package volume to calculate the optimal route. This AI application has resulted in significant savings in time and fuel for UPS.

Conclusion

These case studies illustrate the transformative potential of AI in decision-making across different industries. By providing data-driven insights, predictive analytics, and real-time decision support, AI is helping businesses optimize operations, improve customer satisfaction, reduce costs, and enhance competitiveness.

However, successful AI implementation requires more than just the right technology. It also requires a strategic approach, a culture of data-driven decision-making, and an understanding of the ethical and regulatory implications of AI.

In the next section, we will delve deeper into these considerations and explore how businesses can effectively navigate the challenges and opportunities presented by AI in decision-making. From understanding the limitations of AI to ensuring data privacy and mitigating biases, we'll explore the best practices that businesses should follow to harness the full potential of AI in decision-making.

Whether you're a business leader seeking to implement AI in your organization or a professional aiming to understand how AI can transform your industry, these case studies provide valuable insights into the practical applications of AI in decision-making. They illustrate not just the potential of AI, but also the strategic considerations that go into successful AI implementation.

As we continue our journey into the world of AI-powered decision-making, these case studies serve as a reminder that AI is not just a technology, but a tool that, when used strategically, can drive significant improvements in business performance and decision-making.

The future of business decision-making is here, and it's powered by AI. By understanding and learning from these real-world applications, businesses can better prepare for this new era of AI-driven decision-making, and seize the opportunities it presents for growth, innovation, and competitive advantage.

Chapter 3

AI and Customer Engagement

W

elcome to Chapter 3, where we delve into the exciting realm of Artificial Intelligence (AI) and its impact on customer engagement. In today's hyper-connected and competitive business landscape, customer engagement has become more critical than ever. Businesses that fail to engage their customers risk losing them to competitors who can. This is where AI comes into play, providing new tools and approaches that can significantly enhance customer engagement efforts.

This chapter will explore the various ways in which AI is revolutionizing customer engagement, from personalized marketing and customer service automation to predictive customer behavior and sentiment analysis. We'll examine how AI can help businesses understand their customers better, anticipate their needs, personalize their experiences, and build stronger, more meaningful relationships with them.

Understanding Customer Engagement: A Brief Overview

In the modern business landscape, customer engagement has emerged as a critical factor influencing a company's success. It is no longer sufficient to offer a high-quality product or service; businesses must also actively engage their customers, nurturing lasting relationships and fostering brand loyalty.

What is Customer Engagement?

Customer engagement refers to the emotional connection and relationship that a customer has with a business. It goes beyond a simple transaction or interaction and delves into how a customer feels about a company and its offerings. Engaged customers are not just one-time purchasers; they are repeat buyers, advocates, and ambassadors who promote the brand within their networks.

The Importance of Customer Engagement

In today's competitive business environment, customer engagement is more important than ever. Engaged customers are more likely to be loyal, make repeat purchases, and recommend the brand to others. This loyalty and advocacy can have a significant impact on a business's bottom line, contributing to increased customer lifetime value and higher revenue.

Customer engagement is also a key differentiator in crowded markets. With so many options available to consumers, businesses that successfully engage their customers can stand out from the competition and secure a larger market share.

Customer Engagement Strategies

Effective customer engagement strategies vary depending on the business and its target audience. However, some common strategies include personalizing customer interactions, providing exceptional customer service, creating valuable content, and engaging customers through social media.

One of the most crucial elements of successful customer engagement is personalization. Customers want to feel valued and understood, and personalization helps achieve this by tailoring interactions and offerings to each customer's needs and preferences.

Exceptional customer service is another critical aspect of customer engagement. When customers feel that a business is responsive to their needs and complaints, they are more likely to remain loyal and engaged.

Content creation, whether through blogs, videos, or other formats, is also an effective way to engage customers. High-quality content that is valuable and relevant to customers can attract their attention, keep them engaged with the brand, and foster a sense of community.

Finally, social media is a powerful tool for customer engagement. It allows businesses to interact with customers directly, respond to their comments and feedback, and share content that resonates with them.

Challenges in Customer Engagement

Despite the importance of customer engagement, many businesses struggle to engage their customers effectively. Some common challenges include understanding customer needs and preferences, personalizing interactions at scale, and maintaining consistent engagement across different channels and touchpoints.

To overcome these challenges, businesses often turn to technology. Customer relationship management (CRM) systems, for instance, can help businesses track customer interactions and preferences, enabling more personalized and consistent engagement. Similarly, data analytics tools can provide insights into customer behavior, informing more effective engagement strategies.

The Role of Technology in Customer Engagement

In recent years, technology has dramatically reshaped customer engagement. From CRM systems and data analytics tools to social media platforms and chatbots, technology has enabled businesses to engage customers in new and innovative ways.

One of the most transformative technologies in customer engagement is Artificial Intelligence (AI). AI can analyze vast amounts of data to understand customer behavior, personalize interactions, automate customer service, and more. As we delve deeper into this chapter, we'll explore the various ways AI is revolutionizing customer engagement and reshaping the business landscape.

To conclude, customer engagement is a critical aspect of modern business. By understanding what customer engagement entails, its importance, and the strategies and challenges associated with it, businesses can better navigate the competitive landscape and foster lasting relationships with their customers.

The Role of AI in Enhancing Customer Engagement

Artificial Intelligence (AI) is at the forefront of customer engagement, serving as a catalyst in creating more personalized, efficient, and dynamic interactions between businesses and their customers. Let's unpack how AI is enhancing various facets of customer engagement.

Personalizing Customer Experiences

One of the most significant contributions of AI in customer engagement is personalization. AI algorithms can analyze massive amounts of data in real-time, understanding individual customer preferences, behaviors, and needs. These insights can then be used to deliver personalized messages, product recommendations, or services, creating a unique experience for each customer.

Imagine a retail website that knows your style preferences and can suggest items you might like based on your browsing history, or an email campaign that sends you offers on the products you've shown interest in. These personalized experiences make customers feel valued and understood, improving engagement and building stronger relationships.

Automating Customer Service

AI has revolutionized customer service through automation. Chatbots and virtual assistants, powered by AI, can handle common customer queries 24/7, providing instant responses and freeing up human agents to tackle more complex issues. Not only does this improve efficiency, but it also enhances customer satisfaction as customers can get help anytime, they need.

Moreover, with the ability to learn from past interactions, these AI-powered tools can improve over time, offering more accurate and relevant responses. This constant learning and improvement make AI a valuable tool in enhancing customer service.

Predicting Customer Behavior

AI is capable of predictive analysis, which can be extremely beneficial for customer engagement. By analyzing historical data, AI can predict future customer behaviors, such as purchase patterns or likelihood of churn. These predictions allow businesses to proactively address customer needs, potentially preventing issues before they arise and ensuring customers remain satisfied and engaged.

For instance, if AI predicts a high-value customer is likely to churn based on their recent behavior, a business can take proactive steps to re-engage them, such as offering personalized discounts or reaching out for feedback.

Analyzing Customer Sentiment

AI can analyze text and voice data to understand customer sentiment, a process known as sentiment analysis. By analyzing customer reviews, social media posts, or call center transcripts, AI can determine whether a customer's sentiment towards the brand is positive, negative, or neutral. This information can provide valuable insights into customer satisfaction and highlight areas for improvement.

For example, if sentiment analysis reveals a surge in negative sentiment following a product update, the business can quickly identify and address the issues causing dissatisfaction.

Enhancing Customer Segmentation

Customer segmentation is a crucial marketing strategy that involves dividing a customer base into segments based on characteristics like demographics, behavior, and preferences. AI can enhance this process by analyzing more data points and creating more detailed and accurate customer segments. Businesses can then tailor their engagement strategies to each segment, improving relevance and effectiveness.

Facilitating Omnichannel Engagement

Finally, AI plays a crucial role in enabling omnichannel engagement. By integrating data from various touchpoints, AI can provide a unified view of each customer's interactions with the brand, regardless of channel. This helps businesses deliver a seamless and consistent experience across all channels, which is key to successful customer engagement in today's multi-channel world.

In conclusion, AI is a powerful tool in enhancing customer engagement. By personalizing customer experiences, automating customer service, predicting customer behavior, analyzing customer sentiment, enhancing customer segmentation, and facilitating omnichannel engagement, AI can help businesses engage customers more effectively and build stronger, more meaningful relationships.

AI and Real-Time Engagement

Artificial Intelligence isn't just about analyzing past customer behavior, it's about understanding what customers are doing right now, and responding in real-time. This can be achieved through real-time analytics, which use AI and machine learning to analyze data as it arrives.

For example, if a customer adds an item to their online shopping cart but then seems to abandon it, real-time analytics can trigger an immediate response such as a pop-up chatbot reminding the customer about their item, or a personalized email offering a discount on that product. This immediate engagement can help to bring customers back and complete their purchase, thereby increasing conversion rates.

AI and Customer Retention

AI doesn't just help businesses acquire new customers; it plays a crucial role in retaining existing ones. By using AI to continually engage and delight customers, businesses can increase customer loyalty and reduce churn rates.

One way AI can enhance customer retention is through personalized loyalty programs. AI can analyze individual customer behavior to understand what rewards each customer is likely to find most appealing. This enables businesses to offer personalized rewards, which can be more effective in driving loyalty than one-size-fits-all programs.

AI and Customer Feedback

Collecting customer feedback is crucial for businesses to understand how they can improve. AI can play a significant role in this process, making it easier to collect, analyze, and act on feedback.

AI-powered surveys can adapt based on previous responses, asking more relevant questions, and improving the quality of feedback. Once feedback is collected, AI can analyze it to identify common themes and areas for improvement. This allows businesses to respond to feedback, improving their product or service and enhancing customer satisfaction quickly and effectively.

The Future of AI in Customer Engagement

As AI technology continues to evolve, its role in customer engagement is set to grow even further. Advances in AI will likely lead to more personalized and efficient customer interactions, and new AI technologies could open exciting new possibilities for customer engagement.

One potential future development is the use of AI to create fully personalized customer journeys. AI could analyze each customer's interactions with a business to create a unique journey tailored to their needs and preferences. This could involve personalized product recommendations, content, and even user interfaces, creating a truly unique and engaging experience for each customer.

In conclusion, AI is transforming the world of customer engagement, offering businesses new and exciting ways to connect with their customers. As technology continues to evolve, we can expect AI to play an increasingly important role in shaping the customer experiences of the future.

Case Studies: AI in Customer Engagement

To further understand how AI enhances customer engagement, let's look at real-world examples of companies that have successfully implemented AI in their customer engagement strategies.

Amazon: Personalized Recommendations

Amazon is a prime example of how AI can be used to personalize the customer experience. The company uses AI to analyze individual customer behavior, including their purchase history, items in their shopping cart, items they've rated or reviewed, and what other customers with similar behaviors have purchased.

Based on this analysis, Amazon provides personalized product recommendations, making the shopping experience more relevant and engaging for each customer. This has proven to be incredibly successful, with reports suggesting that 35% of Amazon's sales come from its recommendation engine.

Starbucks: Predictive Analysis

Starbucks uses AI to enhance customer engagement through its mobile app. The app uses predictive analysis to offer personalized product recommendations based on the customer's order history, time of day, and current location.

In addition, Starbucks uses AI to optimize its operational efficiency, such as managing inventory and scheduling staff, to ensure a smooth customer experience. By understanding customer behavior and preferences, Starbucks can provide a more personalized and efficient service, leading to higher customer satisfaction and loyalty.

Spotify: AI-Driven Music Recommendations

Spotify uses AI to analyze user behavior and provide personalized music recommendations. The company's 'Discover Weekly' feature uses AI to create a personalized playlist for each user every week, based on their listening habits and the habits of other users with similar tastes.

This has proven to be a significant feature for customer engagement, with many users reporting that they look forward to their new playlist each week. By using AI to deliver personalized content, Spotify ensures that users stay engaged with their platform.

Sephora: Virtual Artist App

Beauty retailer Sephora has taken customer engagement to the next level with its Virtual Artist App. The app uses AI and Augmented Reality (AR) to allow customers to virtually try on different makeup products.

Customers can see how products look on their own face and experiment with different styles, all from the comfort of their own home. This not only makes the shopping experience more engaging and fun but also helps customers make more informed purchasing decisions.

Bank of America: AI-Powered Virtual Assistant

Bank of America has enhanced its customer service with Erica, an AI-powered virtual assistant. Erica can help customers with a variety of tasks, such as checking balances, scheduling payments, and providing financial advice.

The assistant uses predictive analytics and cognitive messaging to provide personalized financial guidance based on each customer's specific situation. By automating these services with AI, Bank of America can provide a more efficient and personalized service, improving customer engagement and satisfaction.

Netflix: Personalized Content and User Experience

Netflix uses AI to personalize the user experience in multiple ways. It recommends shows and movies based on a user's viewing history, but it also goes a step further. The AI also personalizes the artwork displayed for each title based on the user's preferences.

For example, a user who watches a lot of romance might see a romantic scene from a movie in the thumbnail, while a user who watches a lot of action might see an action-packed scene from the same movie. This level of personalization makes the platform more engaging and keeps users coming back for more.

Zara: AI in Fashion Retail

Zara, one of the world's leading fashion retailers, uses AI to enhance customer engagement and optimize its operations. The company uses AI to analyze customer behavior and fashion trends, enabling it to quickly respond to changing customer demands and stay ahead of the competition.

In addition, Zara uses AI to optimize its supply chain, ensuring that popular items are always in stock and that products are distributed efficiently across its stores. This not only improves operational efficiency but also leads to a better shopping experience for customers.

Lemonade: AI in Insurance

Lemonade, a digital insurance company, uses AI to streamline the insurance process and enhance customer engagement. Customers can purchase insurance policies and file claims through Lemonade's AI-powered chatbot, which uses machine learning to understand customer needs and provide personalized service.

By automating these processes with AI, Lemonade can provide a faster and more efficient service, leading to higher customer satisfaction. This has helped Lemonade to disrupt the traditional insurance market and quickly gain a large customer base.

Grammarly: AI in Writing

Grammarly, a digital writing assistant, uses AI to enhance customer engagement by improving their writing. The tool uses AI to identify and correct grammatical errors, suggest improvements in word choice and style, and even check for plagiarism.

By providing a valuable service that helps users improve their writing, Grammarly keeps its users engaged and loyal to the platform. In addition, Grammarly uses AI to provide personalized writing feedback based on each user's unique writing style and goals, further enhancing the user experience.

Concluding Remarks

In summary, these case studies highlight the transformative impact of AI on customer engagement across various industries. Whether it's personalizing the customer experience, optimizing operations, or providing valuable services, AI offers businesses a powerful tool to engage their customers in new and exciting ways. As AI technology continues to evolve, we can expect to see even more innovative uses of AI in customer engagement in the future.

Challenges and Considerations in AI-Powered Customer Engagement

While AI can significantly enhance customer engagement, implementing it is not without its challenges. Businesses need to be aware of these challenges and carefully consider them when planning their AI strategy.

Data Privacy and Security

One of the main challenges in implementing AI for customer engagement is ensuring data privacy and security. AI systems often rely on large amounts of personal data to function effectively, and this data must be handled responsibly.

Businesses must comply with data protection regulations, such as the General Data Protection Regulation (GDPR) in the European Union and the California Consumer Privacy Act (CCPA) in the United States. Failure to comply with these regulations can result in significant penalties and damage to a company's reputation.

Moreover, customers are becoming increasingly concerned about their data privacy. Businesses must be transparent about how they use and protect customer data to maintain trust and engagement.

Understanding Customer Behavior

While AI can analyze customer behavior and provide valuable insights, understanding the reasons behind this behavior can be challenging. AI systems can identify patterns and correlations, but they cannot explain why these patterns exist.

This means that businesses must combine AI with human understanding to interpret the results effectively. For example, if an AI system identifies that customers are more likely to make a purchase at a particular time, businesses need to understand why this is the case to implement effective strategies.

AI Bias

AI systems learn from the data they are trained on, which means that they can inherit any biases present in this data. This can lead to unfair or discriminatory outcomes, which can damage customer relationships and lead to legal issues.

To prevent AI bias, businesses need to ensure that their training data is diverse and representative. They should also regularly test their AI systems for bias and make any necessary adjustments.

Technological Challenges

Implementing AI can be technically challenging, requiring specialized knowledge and resources. Businesses may need to hire new staff or provide training for existing staff to manage and maintain their AI systems.

Moreover, AI technologies are evolving rapidly, and businesses need to stay up to date with the latest developments to remain competitive. This requires ongoing investment in research and development.

Integration with Existing Systems

AI systems often need to be integrated with existing business systems, such as customer relationship management (CRM) systems, e-commerce platforms, and data analytics tools. This can be complex and time-consuming, and it may require significant changes to existing workflows and processes.

Businesses need to carefully plan their AI implementation to ensure that it integrates smoothly with their existing systems and that all staff are trained on how to use the new technology effectively.

Setting Realistic Expectations

While AI offers many exciting possibilities for customer engagement, it's essential to set realistic expectations. AI is not a magic solution that will solve all business challenges, and it takes time to implement and optimize effectively.

Businesses should set clear goals for their AI initiatives and measure their progress against these goals. They should also be prepared for some trial and error, as it can take time to find the right AI solution for their specific needs.

Conclusion

Implementing AI for customer engagement offers significant potential benefits, but it also comes with challenges. Businesses need to carefully consider these challenges and plan their AI strategy accordingly. By doing so, they can maximize the benefits of AI while minimizing the risks, leading to more effective and engaging customer experiences.

The Future of Customer Engagement with AI

AI has already started to revolutionize customer engagement, but we are still in the early stages of this transformation. Let's explore what the future might hold for AI in customer engagement.

Hyper-Personalization

In the future, AI will enable an unprecedented level of personalization in customer engagement. With AI, businesses will be able to analyze customer data in real-time and use these insights to tailor every aspect of the customer experience to the individual's preferences, behavior, and real-time context.

For example, AI could enable businesses to send personalized product recommendations, offer individualized discounts, or provide personalized customer service based on a customer's previous interactions with the business. This level of personalization will lead to more engaging and satisfying customer experiences.

Omnichannel Engagement

AI will enable businesses to engage customers seamlessly across multiple channels, including online, in-store, on social media, and through mobile apps. This will provide customers with a unified and consistent experience, regardless of how they interact with the business.

AI will also enable businesses to track customer behavior across channels, providing valuable insights that can be used to optimize the customer experience. For example, a business could use AI to identify when a customer is likely to switch channels and ensure that the transition is seamless.

Voice and Visual Search

With advancements in AI technology, voice and visual search are set to become increasingly prevalent. Voice assistants like Amazon's Alexa and Google's Assistant are already popular, and their capabilities are set to expand significantly in the future.

Similarly, visual search technology, which allows users to search for products by taking a photo, is set to become more widespread. These technologies will provide new ways for businesses to engage with customers and will require businesses to adapt their strategies accordingly.

Predictive Engagement

AI will enable businesses to anticipate customer needs and engage with them proactively. For example, an AI system could analyze a customer's previous interactions and predict when they might need assistance, allowing the business to provide support before the customer even asks for it.

Predictive engagement could also be used in marketing, with AI predicting which products or services a customer is likely to be interested in and promoting these products proactively.

Emotion AI

Emotion AI, also known as affective computing, involves AI systems that can recognize, interpret, and respond to human emotions. In the context of customer engagement, emotion AI could be used to understand how customers are feeling and adjust the interaction accordingly.

For example, if a customer is frustrated, an AI system could recognize this and adapt its responses to help calm the customer. This could lead to more empathetic and effective customer interactions.

Augmented Reality (AR) and Virtual Reality (VR)

AR and VR technologies are set to become increasingly integrated with AI in the future, providing new ways for businesses to engage with customers. For example, a retailer could use AR and AI to enable customers to virtually try on clothes, while a travel company could use VR and AI to provide virtual tours of holiday destinations.

Conclusion

In conclusion, the future of customer engagement with AI looks incredibly exciting. With advancements in technology, we can expect AI to become even more integrated into our daily lives, providing businesses with new and innovative ways to engage with their customers. However, as with any technological advancement, it's essential for businesses to consider the ethical implications and ensure that they use AI in a way that respects customer privacy and promotes fairness and transparency.

Chapter 4

Innovating Business Models with AI

W

elcome to Chapter 4, where we delve into the exciting world of AI-driven business model innovation. As the fourth industrial revolution unfolds, Artificial Intelligence (AI) has taken the center stage, opening new opportunities and challenges for businesses around the globe. It is fundamentally changing the way we live, work, and conduct business. In this ever-evolving landscape, adapting to the AI revolution is not a matter of choice but a necessity for survival and success.

In this chapter, we will explore how AI is transforming traditional business models, fostering innovation, and driving competitive advantage. We will uncover how AI can serve as a potent tool for creating and capturing value in novel ways and how companies can rethink their strategic approach to leverage AI capabilities effectively.

Business models are fundamental frameworks that outline how an organization creates, delivers, and captures value. With the advent of AI, these models are undergoing significant changes. The transformative power of AI lies in its ability to redefine value propositions, transform value chains, and change profit formulas, leading to the development of innovative business models.

We'll start by understanding the concept of a business model and how AI can play a crucial role in redefining it. We will then move on to examine the different ways in which AI is being used to drive business model innovation across various sectors. We'll look at real-world case studies that highlight the successful integration of AI into business models.

In addition, we'll discuss the challenges associated with implementing AI-driven business models, including the ethical implications, data privacy concerns, and the need for regulatory compliance. Finally, we will explore the future potential of AI in shaping business models and offer some insights into how businesses can prepare for this exciting future.

This chapter aims to provide a comprehensive understanding of how AI can be a catalyst for business model innovation. Whether you're an entrepreneur, a business leader, or a manager, the insights offered in this chapter will equip you with the knowledge to navigate the exciting terrain of AI-driven business model innovation. Let's embark on this journey together!

How AI Transforms Business Models

Artificial Intelligence (AI) is not merely a new technology that businesses can add to their toolkit. Its implications are far-reaching, permeating every level of business operations, and even altering the very structures upon which businesses are built. To understand the transformative effect of AI, we need to first understand the concept of a business model and then see how AI can change these models fundamentally.

Understanding Business Models

A business model outlines how a company creates, delivers, and captures value. It's the blueprint of a company's strategy for success, incorporating elements such as value propositions, customer segments, channels, customer relationships, key activities, key resources, key partners, cost structures, and revenue streams. A successful business model is one that can effectively identify a customer's need and fulfill it in a profitable way.

AI as a Catalyst for Change

AI is a game-changer for business models because it opens up new ways for businesses to create and deliver value. By harnessing the power of AI, businesses can develop deeper insights about their customers, automate routine tasks, enhance decision-making, and offer innovative products and services that were previously unimaginable. This radical transformation happens in several ways.

AI and Value Creation

AI enables businesses to create value in new and innovative ways. By leveraging AI, businesses can develop personalized products and services that cater to individual customer needs. With AI's predictive capabilities, businesses can anticipate customer needs and fulfill them proactively. Moreover, AI-powered products and services often carry a novelty factor that can create a unique value proposition, giving businesses a competitive edge.

AI and Value Delivery

AI also transforms how businesses deliver value. Traditional business models are often linear, with value flowing from the producer to the consumer. However, AI enables a more dynamic, interconnected value delivery system. For instance, businesses can use AI to analyze data from multiple touchpoints in real-time, allowing them to adjust their offerings on the fly based on immediate customer feedback. This creates a more responsive and customer-centric value delivery model.

AI and Value Capture

Finally, AI can significantly impact how businesses capture value. With AI, businesses can implement dynamic pricing models that can optimize revenue based on demand, competition, and customer behavior. Moreover, AI can help businesses identify the most profitable customer segments and tailor their marketing efforts accordingly.

Real-World Examples

Companies like Netflix and Amazon provide excellent examples of AI-driven business model innovation. Netflix leverages AI to personalize recommendations for its users, creating a unique value proposition. Amazon uses AI to optimize its logistics and supply chain, ensuring efficient value delivery. Both companies use AI to understand customer behavior better, allowing them to capture value effectively.

The Shift towards AI-centric Business Models

As AI continues to evolve, we are witnessing a shift towards AI-centric business models. In these models, AI is not just a tool but a core component of the business strategy. Companies like Google, Tesla, and DeepMind are leading this shift, with business models built around AI's capabilities.

Conclusion

In conclusion, AI is not just transforming existing business models but also creating entirely new ones. By reshaping value creation, delivery, and capture, AI offers businesses the opportunity to innovate and gain a competitive edge. However, the transition to an AI-driven business model is not without its challenges. Businesses need to navigate complex issues related to data privacy, ethics, and regulation.

Furthermore, successfully implementing an AI-driven business model requires a deep understanding of AI and a willingness to embrace change.

Case Studies: AI and Business Model Innovation

AI has already demonstrated its potential to radically transform business models across various industries. In this section, we will delve into a few illustrative case studies from diverse sectors that showcase the significant impact of AI on business model innovation.

Netflix: Personalized Entertainment

Netflix is a prime example of how AI can transform a business model. The company started as a DVD-by-mail service, but it was the shift to a digital streaming platform powered by AI that truly catapulted Netflix to global success. The company uses AI to analyze vast amounts of data about viewers' watching habits, ratings, and reviews. This information is used to provide personalized recommendations, creating a unique value proposition for customers. In addition, Netflix uses AI to make strategic decisions about content creation and acquisition. This AI-driven business model has not only helped Netflix retain its customer base but also to grow it exponentially.

Amazon: AI-driven E-commerce

Amazon's success story is another testament to AI's transformative power. The company started as an online bookseller but quickly expanded its product range. Today, Amazon is a global e-commerce giant, and AI plays a pivotal role in its business model. Amazon uses AI for various purposes, from recommending products based on customer preferences to predicting future demand for efficient inventory management. Amazon's AI-powered voice assistant, Alexa, has also created a new market segment for the company. These AI applications have helped Amazon deliver superior customer experiences and achieve operational excellence.

Tesla: Revolutionizing the Auto Industry

Tesla is a classic example of an AI-centric business model. The company's mission is to accelerate the world's transition to sustainable energy. To achieve this, Tesla leverages AI in various aspects of its business model. The most notable application is in its self-driving technology. Tesla's vehicles continuously collect data while they're on the road, which is then used to improve the company's autonomous driving algorithms. This AI-driven approach has enabled Tesla to remain at the forefront of the electric vehicle market.

Stitch Fix: AI-powered Fashion

Stitch Fix is an online personal styling service that uses AI to disrupt the traditional retail model. Customers provide information about their style, size, and price preferences. Stitch Fix's AI algorithms analyze this data, along with broader fashion trends, to provide personalized clothing recommendations. Human stylists then curate a selection of clothes that are shipped to the customer. This AI-driven business model allows Stitch Fix to offer a personalized shopping experience on a large scale, a value proposition that sets it apart in the competitive fashion industry.

Zebra Medical Vision: AI in Healthcare

Zebra Medical Vision is an Israeli startup that uses AI to read medical imaging scans. The company's AI algorithms can detect a range of diseases, from liver disease to lung cancer, with a high degree of accuracy. This AI-driven business model allows Zebra Medical Vision to provide a valuable service to healthcare providers, helping them diagnose diseases more quickly and accurately.

Conclusion

These case studies highlight the transformative potential of AI across various industries. From entertainment and e-commerce to the automotive and healthcare sectors, AI is driving business model innovation by offering new ways to create, deliver, and capture value. However, it's important to note that these companies' success is not merely a result of using AI but also of integrating it strategically into their business models. The shift to an AI-driven business model requires a deep understanding of AI's capabilities and limitations, a clear vision, and a willingness to challenge the status quo.

Chapter 5
Understanding AI Technologies

W

elcome to Chapter 5: "Understanding AI Technologies." This chapter delves into the core technologies that form the backbone of artificial intelligence systems. It provides an overview of the different types of AI technologies and their unique features, shedding light on how these technologies are leveraged in various business contexts to drive innovation, efficiency, and growth.

Understanding AI technologies is crucial for business leaders, decision-makers, and even individuals in non-technical roles. It enables us to comprehend the potential and limitations of AI, make informed decisions about AI implementation, and foresee the upcoming trends and possibilities in the AI landscape.

In this chapter, we'll discuss key AI technologies such as Machine Learning, Deep Learning, Natural Language Processing, Computer Vision, Robotics Process Automation, and more. We will explore how these technologies function, their various applications, and their transformative potential across industries. We will also touch upon the ethical considerations and challenges linked with these technologies, providing a balanced and comprehensive view of the AI tech ecosystem.

By the end of this chapter, you'll have a solid foundation in AI technologies, equipping you with the knowledge to harness the power of AI in your business or field effectively. Let's begin our journey into the fascinating world of AI technologies.

Machine Learning

Machine Learning (ML) is a subset of artificial intelligence that focuses on building systems capable of learning from data and making predictions or decisions without being explicitly programmed to do so. It is the driving force behind many of the AI applications we see today, from recommendation systems on Netflix and Amazon to voice recognition software like Siri and Alexa.

What is Machine Learning?

Machine learning is based on algorithms that can learn from and make decisions based on data. These algorithms are designed to improve over time by being exposed to more data, allowing them to adapt when exposed to new data.

There are several types of machine learning, including supervised learning, unsupervised learning, semi-supervised learning, and reinforcement learning.

In supervised learning, the algorithm learns from a labeled dataset to make predictions. For instance, an algorithm might be trained on a dataset of patient information to predict whether they have a particular disease. The 'label' is whether the patient has the disease.

Unsupervised learning, in contrast, involves training an algorithm on a dataset without labels. The algorithm must find patterns and relationships within the data. This type is often used for clustering and association tasks, such as customer segmentation in marketing.

Semi-supervised learning is a mix of supervised and unsupervised learning. It involves using a small amount of labeled data with a large amount of unlabeled data. This method is beneficial when acquiring labeled data requires significant resources.

Reinforcement learning is a type of machine learning where an agent learns to behave in an environment, by performing actions and seeing the results. This type is extensively used in playing games, robotics, and navigation.

Applications of Machine Learning

Machine learning is used in a vast array of applications today. Some common uses of machine learning include:

Predictive Analytics: Many businesses use machine learning for predictive analytics, which involves using historical data to predict future events. It can be used to forecast sales, anticipate maintenance needs, or predict stock market trends.

Personalization: Machine learning powers the personalized experiences we encounter every day on the internet. From product recommendations on e-commerce websites to personalized playlists on music streaming services, machine learning algorithms use data about a user's behavior to tailor their experience.

Fraud Detection: Banks and other financial institutions use machine learning to detect fraudulent activity. Machine learning algorithms can analyze millions of transactions in real-time, identifying patterns that could indicate fraud.

Natural Language Processing (NLP): Machine learning is the backbone of NLP, which allows computers to understand, interpret, and generate human language. NLP powers virtual assistants, chatbots, and translation software.

Image Recognition: Machine learning is used in computer vision, a field that enables computers to interpret and understand visual information from the world. It powers technologies like facial recognition and autonomous vehicles.

The Future of Machine Learning

The future of machine learning is incredibly promising. As more data becomes available and machine learning algorithms become more sophisticated, we can expect to see even more innovative applications of machine learning. For instance, machine learning could play a key role in healthcare, helping to predict disease outbreaks or personalize medical treatments.

However, as machine learning continues to evolve, it also brings certain challenges. One of the main challenges is the 'black box' problem – it's often difficult to understand how machine learning algorithms make decisions, which can lead to issues with transparency and accountability. There are also concerns about privacy and data security, as machine learning often relies on large amounts of data.

In conclusion, machine learning is a crucial component of artificial intelligence, powering many of the AI applications we see today. By understanding machine learning – what it is, how it works, and where it's going, we can harness its potential and navigate the challenges ahead. As researchers and experts continue to push the boundaries of machine learning, advancements in interpretability and explainability are being made to address the 'black box' problem. Efforts are underway to develop methods that provide insights into how machine learning models arrive at their decisions, ensuring transparency and accountability.

Moreover, the development of privacy-preserving techniques and robust data protection measures is critical to maintaining trust in machine learning systems. Striking the right balance between data utilization and privacy safeguards will be essential in the future of machine learning.

As we look ahead, collaboration between domain experts, data scientists, and policymakers will be crucial. Together, they can shape regulations and ethical frameworks that guide the responsible and beneficial use of machine learning technologies.

With the continued advancements in machine learning, we can expect it to revolutionize various industries, drive innovation, and improve decision-making processes. By staying informed and adapting to emerging trends, we can make the most of the boundless possibilities that lie in the future of machine learning.

Deep Learning

Deep Learning is a subfield of machine learning that focuses on neural networks with many layers, also known as deep neural networks. These networks are designed to mimic the way the human brain works, enabling machines to learn and process complex information. Deep learning has seen tremendous growth in recent years, thanks to advances in computing power and the availability of large datasets.

What is Deep Learning?

Deep learning is a specialized form of machine learning that uses artificial neural networks to model and solve problems. These neural networks consist of layers of interconnected nodes or neurons that process and transmit information. The more layers a neural network has, the deeper it is, and the more complex patterns it can learn.

Deep learning networks can automatically learn to extract features from raw data, such as images or text, without human intervention. This ability to learn hierarchical feature representations sets deep learning apart from traditional machine learning, which often relies on manual feature engineering.

There are various types of deep learning architectures, including Convolutional Neural Networks (CNNs), Recurrent Neural Networks (RNNs), and Generative Adversarial Networks (GANs), each with their unique strengths and applications.

Applications of Deep Learning

Deep learning has a wide range of applications across various industries. Some of the most common applications include:

Computer Vision: Deep learning has revolutionized computer vision, allowing machines to recognize and classify objects in images and videos with high accuracy. Convolutional Neural Networks (CNNs) are a popular deep learning architecture used for image recognition tasks, such as facial recognition and autonomous vehicle navigation.

Natural Language Processing (NLP): Deep learning has significantly advanced the field of NLP, enabling machines to better understand, interpret, and generate human language. Recurrent Neural Networks (RNNs) and Transformer models are commonly used for NLP tasks, such as machine translation, sentiment analysis, and text summarization.

Speech Recognition: Deep learning has improved the accuracy and efficiency of speech recognition systems, which convert spoken language into written text. This technology is used in voice assistants like Siri, Alexa, and Google Assistant, as well as transcription services and call center automation.

Generative Models: Deep learning can be used to create generative models, which can generate new, realistic data samples based on existing data. Generative Adversarial Networks (GANs) are a popular deep learning architecture for tasks like image synthesis, style transfer, and data augmentation.

Reinforcement Learning: Deep learning can be combined with reinforcement learning, a type of machine learning where an agent learns to make decisions by interacting with an environment. This approach, known as Deep Reinforcement Learning, has been successful in training AI agents to play games like Go and StarCraft II at a superhuman level.

The Future of Deep Learning

The future of deep learning is incredibly exciting, with new techniques and applications continually emerging. As computing power continues to increase, and more data becomes available, deep learning models will become more sophisticated and capable of solving even more complex problems.

One of the key challenges for the future of deep learning is the need for large amounts of labeled data to train models. This can be resource-intensive and time-consuming, particularly for tasks that require expert knowledge. However, advances in techniques like unsupervised learning, semi-supervised learning, and transfer learning may help overcome this challenge by reducing the need for labeled data.

Another challenge is the interpretability of deep learning models. Like other machine learning models, deep learning models can be difficult to understand and explain, raising concerns about transparency and accountability. Researchers are working on techniques to improve the explainability of deep learning models, which could make them more accessible and trustworthy. Ethical considerations are also increasingly important in the field of deep learning. As these models are used in more decision-making processes, the potential for bias, discrimination, and privacy violations becomes a significant concern. It's essential to develop and implement strategies for ethical AI use, including fairness, accountability, transparency, and privacy protection.

Despite these challenges, deep learning holds immense potential. It's expected to drive significant advancements in fields like healthcare, where it can be used for early disease detection and personalized medicine, and in autonomous vehicles, where it can enable safer and more efficient transportation. It's also anticipated that deep learning will play a crucial role in the development of artificial general intelligence (AGI), a form of AI that can understand, learn, and apply its intelligence to any intellectual task that a human being can do.

Deep Learning and Business

For businesses, deep learning offers opportunities to gain a competitive edge, improve customer experiences, and optimize operations. For instance, deep learning algorithms can help companies better understand their customers by analyzing vast amounts of data from various sources, such as social media, customer reviews, and transaction history. This can lead to more effective marketing strategies, improved customer service, and more personalized customer experiences.

In operations, deep learning can be used to predict maintenance needs, optimize supply chains, and improve quality control. These applications can lead to significant cost savings and efficiency improvements.

However, integrating deep learning into business processes is not without its challenges. It requires significant technical expertise, substantial computational resources, and access to large amounts of data. Moreover, businesses need to navigate regulatory and ethical considerations when using AI.

In conclusion, deep learning is a powerful tool with the potential to transform various aspects of society, from business and healthcare to transportation and entertainment. By understanding deep learning – what it is, how it works, and where it's going – we can better prepare for a future where AI plays an increasingly significant role.

Natural Language Processing

Natural Language Processing (NLP) is a branch of artificial intelligence that focuses on the interaction between computers and humans through natural language. The ultimate goal of NLP is to read, decipher, understand, and make sense of the human language in a valuable way.

What is Natural Language Processing?

Natural Language Processing is a discipline that focuses on the interaction between data science and human language, and it's scaling to lots of industries. Today NLP is booming thanks to the huge improvements in the access to data and the increase in computational power, which are allowing practitioners to achieve meaningful results in areas like healthcare, media, finance, and human resources among others.

NLP enables computers to analyze, understand, and derive meaning from human language in a smart and useful way. By utilizing NLP, developers can organize and structure knowledge to perform tasks such as automatic summarization, translation, named entity recognition, relationship extraction, sentiment analysis, speech recognition, and topic segmentation.

Applications of Natural Language Processing

NLP can be found in several applications we use daily:

Search Engines: Google, Bing, and other search engines use NLP to understand and deliver relevant results. Autocomplete and spell check are simple examples of NLP in action.

Virtual Assistants: Siri, Alexa, Google Assistant, and Cortana are all proficient in speech recognition thanks to NLP. They can understand spoken language, interpret it, and respond in a way that mimics human conversation.

Sentiment Analysis: Brands and marketers use NLP to monitor public sentiment about their products and services. They analyze online conversations and reviews to understand customer experiences and feedback.

Machine Translation: Services like Google Translate employ NLP to automatically translate text or speech from one language to another.

Spam Detection: Email providers use NLP to filter out spam based on the content of an email.

Automated Resume Screening: Human Resources departments often use NLP algorithms to scan resumes and job descriptions to find the best matches.

The Future of Natural Language Processing

The future of NLP is likely to see even more sophisticated language understanding capabilities. One of the significant challenges that NLP faces is understanding the nuances and context of human language. Sarcasm, humor, slang, and regional dialects all present unique challenges to NLP algorithms. The future of NLP will likely involve improved understanding of these aspects of language.

More advanced NLP models will also likely be able to generate more human-like text. As models are trained on more and more data, their understanding of language improves, and they can generate more realistic, coherent text.

Natural Language Processing and Business

The application of NLP in business is vast and growing. Customer service is one of the areas where NLP is making a significant impact. AI chatbots and virtual assistants use NLP to understand customer queries and provide relevant information or solutions. This not only improves the customer experience by providing immediate assistance but also reduces the workload of customer service representatives.

In the HR domain, NLP is being used to automate the process of resume screening. It can also be used to analyze employee feedback and identify common themes or areas of concern.

Marketing and sales teams can use NLP to analyze social media chatter and customer reviews to gain insights into customer sentiment and preferences. This can inform product development, marketing campaigns, and sales strategies.

In conclusion, NLP is a rapidly evolving field that holds immense potential for business applications. As advancements in AI and machine learning continue, we can expect to see even more sophisticated language understanding capabilities, opening new possibilities for human-computer interaction.

Computer Vision

Computer Vision is a fascinating subfield of artificial intelligence that trains computers to interpret and understand the visual world. By digitally processing, analyzing, and understanding images, machines can automate tasks that require visual cognition. However, the science of computer vision seeks not only to duplicate the abilities of human vision by closely modeling human physiology and perception, but also to go beyond by creating machines that can enhance human abilities or assist in solving difficult problems.

What is Computer Vision?

The field of computer vision is focused on replicating parts of the complexity of the human vision and enabling computers to identify and process objects in images and videos in the same way that humans do. Until recently, computer vision only worked in limited capacity. However, thanks to advances in artificial intelligence and innovations in deep learning and neural networks, the field has been able to take great leaps in recent years and has been able to surpass humans in some tasks related to detecting and labeling objects.

Applications of Computer Vision

Computer vision is used in a variety of sectors. Here are a few:

Autonomous Vehicles: Self-driving cars use computer vision for object detection, navigation, and control. They need to identify objects, such as traffic lights, pedestrians, and other vehicles, to navigate safely.

Healthcare: Computer vision can help doctors to diagnose diseases by automating the analysis of medical images, including MRI scans, CT scans, and X-rays.

Manufacturing: In production lines, computer vision can inspect products to ensure they meet quality standards. It can identify defects or irregularities that may be missed by human inspectors.

Retail: Some stores use computer vision to track inventory, generate heat maps of customer traffic, or even allow customers to make purchases without a traditional checkout process.

Agriculture: Computer vision is used in precision farming to monitor crop health, identify pests or diseases, and optimize resource usage.

The Future of Computer Vision

As technology advances, so too will the capabilities of computer vision. We can expect more sophisticated object detection, facial recognition, gesture recognition, and even emotion recognition. Improved algorithms will be able to better identify and categorize objects, even in complex scenes with multiple overlapping objects.

In the future, we may see computer vision incorporated into more aspects of daily life, such as smart homes that can recognize occupants and adjust settings according to individual preferences. We may also see more widespread use of augmented reality, which relies on computer vision to blend digital content with the real world.

Computer Vision and Business

Businesses stand to benefit significantly from the advancements in computer vision. Retailers can use it to analyze customer behavior, optimize store layouts, and manage inventory. In manufacturing, computer vision can improve quality control and enhance safety by identifying potential hazards. In agriculture, it can boost yields and reduce costs by enabling more precise farming practices.

Despite the potential benefits, implementing computer vision comes with its challenges. It requires significant computational power and expertise in AI and machine learning. Furthermore, privacy concerns may arise when systems can identify individuals or tracking behavior.

In conclusion, computer vision is a rapidly advancing field that is transforming industries and our daily lives. By understanding the basics of computer vision, its applications, and its future trajectory, businesses and individuals can better prepare for a future where machines can see and understand the world around us.

Chapter 6

AI Implementation: Challenges and Solutions

I

n the journey of artificial intelligence, it's not all smooth sailing. Despite its tremendous potential, implementing AI in a business setting comes with its own set of challenges. This chapter, "AI Implementation: Challenges and Solutions," aims to shed light on these issues and offers practical solutions to overcome them.

We start the chapter by exploring the common hurdles organizations encounter when adopting AI. These challenges can range from lack of data and technical expertise to ethical considerations, and resistance to change. Understanding these challenges is the first step towards devising effective strategies to overcome them.

Next, we delve into the specific solutions to address each of these challenges. We provide practical tips, strategies, and best practices that have been effective for various organizations in their AI implementation journey. Whether it's building an in-house AI team, partnering with an AI firm, or adopting AI as a Service, we explore the different ways businesses can acquire the necessary technical expertise. In terms of data, we discuss the importance of data management, data privacy, and using synthetic data.

We also address the ethical considerations in AI implementation, focusing on the importance of transparency, fairness, privacy, and accountability. We highlight the need for AI governance and ethics guidelines to ensure the responsible use of AI.

Lastly, we discuss how to manage the human aspect of AI implementation - dealing with resistance to change. We emphasize the importance of communication, training, and change management strategies to ensure smooth AI adoption.

In essence, this chapter provides a comprehensive guide to navigating the challenges of AI implementation and paves the way for successful AI adoption. We hope that this chapter will equip businesses with the necessary knowledge and tools to overcome the hurdles they might face in their AI journey, and ultimately reap the immense benefits that AI has to offer.

Identifying the Challenges

Implementing artificial intelligence (AI) into a business is not without its challenges. From data management to ethical concerns, understanding these potential roadblocks is crucial to successfully integrating AI into your operations.

Lack of Understanding and Expertise

One of the most common challenges in implementing AI is a lack of understanding of the technology and its potential applications. Many decision-makers do not fully grasp what AI is or how it can be leveraged in their specific business context. This knowledge gap can lead to unrealistic expectations or misuse of technology.

Moreover, there is often a lack of technical expertise needed to develop and maintain AI systems. The field of AI requires specialized skills and knowledge, including proficiency in programming languages like Python, understanding of machine learning algorithms, and experience in working with large datasets. The demand for AI talent significantly outpaces the supply, making it difficult for companies to find and retain qualified personnel.

Data Management Challenges

AI systems require large amounts of high-quality data to learn and make accurate predictions. However, many businesses struggle with data management. They might not have enough data, or the data they do have could be fragmented across different systems, unstructured, or of poor quality.

In addition, businesses must navigate data privacy regulations, such as the General Data Protection Regulation (GDPR) in Europe or the California Consumer Privacy Act (CCPA) in the United States. Ensuring compliance while also utilizing data for AI can be a complex task.

Ethical Considerations

Ethical considerations are another significant challenge in AI implementation. AI systems can potentially introduce bias, infringe on privacy, or make decisions that are not transparent or explainable, which raises concerns about fairness, accountability, and trust.

Moreover, the use of AI can impact employment. While AI can automate routine tasks and free up humans to engage in more complex tasks, it can also lead to job displacement, requiring strategies for reskilling or upskilling workers.

Resistance to Change

Implementing AI often involves significant changes in business processes, organizational structures, and work roles. Such changes can encounter resistance from employees due to fear of job loss, concerns about transparency, or discomfort with new technologies. Managing this change effectively is crucial to successful AI adoption.

High Costs

Developing, implementing, and maintaining AI systems can be costly. Expenses can include not only the development of AI applications but also investment in infrastructure, data management, and hiring or training AI specialists. Smaller businesses or those in the early stages of digital transformation might find these costs prohibitive.

Regulatory Hurdles

Finally, the regulatory landscape for AI is complex and evolving. Regulations can differ by country, state, or industry, and they often struggle to keep pace with the rapid advances in AI technology. Businesses must stay abreast of these regulations to avoid potential legal and reputational risks.

In summary, while AI holds tremendous potential for businesses, its implementation is not a straightforward task. It requires a deep understanding of the technology, careful planning, and thoughtful consideration of various challenges. By identifying these challenges upfront, businesses can better plan their AI strategy and increase their chances of successful implementation. The following sections will delve deeper into these challenges and explore potential solutions to each.

Finding Effective Solutions

Successfully implementing AI in a business setting is about more than merely understanding the technology. It also involves navigating the various challenges and finding effective solutions. This section will delve deeper into possible solutions for the issues identified in the previous section.

Building AI Literacy and Recruiting Talent

Addressing the lack of understanding and technical expertise starts with fostering AI literacy within the organization. This includes educating decision-makers and employees about what AI is, its potential applications, and its limitations. This knowledge allows for realistic expectations and informed decision-making about AI projects.

In terms of technical expertise, businesses have several options. They can invest in training existing employees, hiring new talent, or outsource AI development to third-party firms or consultants. Each approach has its pros and cons, and the choice often depends on the specific business context and resources.

Enhancing Data Management and Ensuring Privacy

Effective data management is crucial for AI success. This involves centralizing and structuring data, improving data quality, and implementing robust data governance practices. Tools and platforms for data management, such as data warehouses, data lakes, and data governance software, can facilitate this process.

Privacy concerns should also be addressed upfront. Businesses should familiarize themselves with relevant data privacy regulations and implement practices to ensure compliance. This may include anonymizing data, obtaining explicit consent for data use, and implementing secure data storage and transfer mechanisms.

Navigating Ethical Considerations

Addressing ethical considerations in AI involves developing and implementing AI ethics guidelines. These guidelines should cover issues such as fairness, transparency, privacy, and accountability. External auditing can also be beneficial to ensure ethical AI practices.

When it comes to job displacement due to AI, businesses should consider strategies for reskilling or upskilling affected workers. This might involve training programs, education initiatives, or job rotation schemes.

Managing Change

Managing the human aspect of AI implementation is crucial. This involves clear communication about the benefits and implications of AI, addressing employee concerns, and providing training for new systems and processes. Changing management strategies and frameworks can be instrumental in facilitating this process.

Balancing Costs

While AI can be costly, it's important to balance these costs against the potential benefits. This involves conducting a thorough cost-benefit analysis and considering not just the immediate costs but also the potential long-term savings and revenue opportunities.

For businesses with limited resources, there are options to lower the costs. For example, AI as a Service (AIaaS) allows businesses to access AI capabilities without the need to develop them in-house. Open-source tools and platforms also provide low-cost alternatives for AI development.

Navigating Regulatory Hurdles

Keeping up with the regulatory landscape for AI requires staying informed about current and upcoming regulations in your region and industry. Legal counsel may be necessary to interpret these regulations and their implications for your AI projects. Joining industry associations or regulatory bodies can also provide valuable insights and updates.

In summary, finding effective solutions for AI implementation challenges involves a combination of education, strategic planning, and careful consideration of ethical, human, and legal factors. By taking a proactive and thoughtful approach, businesses can successfully navigate these challenges and harness the power of AI for their benefit.

Adopting a Pilot-First Approach

One of the most effective ways to overcome the challenges in AI implementation is to adopt a pilot-first approach. Instead of a full-scale roll-out, businesses can start with smaller, pilot projects that allow them to test the waters, learn from their experiences, and gradually scale up. This approach can reduce risk, manage costs, and provide valuable learning opportunities for future AI initiatives.

Building a Collaborative Culture

Successfully implementing AI is not just a technological endeavor; it also requires a shift in culture. Building a collaborative culture where different teams work together to understand and implement AI can be beneficial. This includes fostering a culture of continuous learning and openness to change, which are crucial in the fast-paced world of AI.

Establishing Strong Leadership

Strong leadership is essential for successful AI implementation. Leaders should drive the AI vision, support the necessary cultural shift, and ensure alignment between AI initiatives and business strategy. They should also foster a culture of transparency and trust, as these are key to managing the human aspect of AI implementation.

Involving Stakeholders

Involving all relevant stakeholders in the AI journey is crucial. This includes not only decision-makers and technical teams but also end-users and those who will be affected by the AI systems. Their insights can provide valuable input into the design and implementation of AI systems, and their buy-in can facilitate smoother adoption.

Continuous Monitoring and Improvement

Finally, AI implementation is not a one-off process but a continuous journey. It involves continuous monitoring of AI systems, assessing their performance and impact, and making necessary adjustments. This ongoing process of evaluation and improvement is key to ensuring that AI systems remain effective, relevant, and aligned with business goals.

In conclusion, while the challenges of AI implementation are considerable, they are not insurmountable. By adopting a strategic and thoughtful approach, businesses can navigate these challenges and successfully harness the power of AI. The potential rewards – in terms of efficiency, innovation, and competitiveness – make this journey well worth the effort.

Chapter 7

Building an AI Strategy

I

n the preceding chapters, we've delved into understanding AI, its various applications in business, and the challenges that come with implementing it. However, to truly harness the power of AI, an organization needs a comprehensive AI strategy. This chapter aims to guide you through the process of building an effective AI strategy.

An AI strategy provides a clear roadmap for integrating AI into your business operations. It aligns AI initiatives with business objectives, ensures efficient use of resources, and guides decision-making throughout the AI implementation journey. However, building an AI strategy is not a one-size-fits-all process. It requires a nuanced understanding of your business context, your AI capabilities, and your strategic objectives.

In this chapter, we will explore various components of an AI strategy, from understanding your business needs and defining your AI vision to developing AI capabilities and managing change. We will also delve into topics such as ethical considerations in AI strategy, measuring AI success, and the role of leadership in driving the AI strategy.

Whether you're a business leader seeking to spearhead AI initiatives in your organization or an AI enthusiast wanting to understand the strategic aspects of AI, this chapter will provide you with the insights and guidance you need. So, let's embark on the journey of building an effective AI strategy.

Why Do You Need an AI Strategy?

In the digital age, where technology is rapidly advancing and transforming the business landscape, Artificial Intelligence (AI) has emerged as a key driver of innovation and competitive advantage. Its potential applications are vast, spanning various industries and functions, from improving customer service to streamlining supply chains and enhancing decision-making. However, harnessing the power of AI is not simply about adopting the latest technologies; it requires a strategic approach. This is where an AI strategy comes into play.

Aligning AI Initiatives with Business Objectives

Firstly, an AI strategy is crucial for aligning AI initiatives with business objectives. While AI can offer numerous possibilities, not all of them may be relevant or beneficial to your specific business context. An AI strategy helps you identify and prioritize the AI applications that will deliver the most value to your business, ensuring that your AI investments are aligned with your strategic goals and contribute to your bottom line.

Managing Resources Efficiently

Secondly, developing and implementing AI solutions require significant resources, including time, talent, and financial investment. Without a clear strategy, there's a risk of wasting resources on initiatives that don't yield substantial results or duplicating efforts across different parts of the organization. An AI strategy provides a roadmap for allocating resources efficiently and effectively, maximizing the return on your AI investments.

Navigating the AI Landscape

The world of AI is vast and rapidly evolving, with new technologies, tools, and practices emerging regularly. Navigating this landscape can be overwhelming, especially for businesses that are new to AI. An AI strategy helps you stay on top of these developments, guiding your decision-making and ensuring that your AI initiatives are grounded in the latest knowledge and best practices.

Managing Risks and Ethical Considerations

AI also comes with various risks and ethical considerations, from data privacy issues to the potential for algorithmic bias. An AI strategy is critical for managing these risks effectively. It helps you establish a framework for ethical AI use, including clear guidelines for data management, robust measures for ensuring fairness and transparency in AI systems, and a mechanism for addressing any ethical issues that arise.

Driving Change and Adoption

Finally, implementing AI often involves significant change within the organization, from new processes and systems to new roles and ways of working. An AI strategy is crucial for managing this change effectively and driving the adoption of AI. It provides a clear vision for AI in the organization, outlines the steps for achieving this vision, and guides communication and training efforts to ensure that all stakeholders are onboard and equipped to leverage AI.

In conclusion, an AI strategy is not a luxury but a necessity for businesses seeking to leverage AI. It's the compass that guides your AI journey, ensuring that your AI initiatives are purposeful, efficient, up-to-date, ethical, and well-received. Without a clear AI strategy, businesses run the risk of missing the mark with their AI initiatives, wasting valuable resources, or even running afoul of ethical and regulatory standards. Therefore, understanding why you need an AI strategy and how to build one effectively is a critical step in your AI journey. In the following sections, we will delve deeper into the key components of an AI strategy and provide guidance on how to build one.

Developing an Effective AI Strategy

While understanding the importance of an AI strategy is crucial, translating this understanding into a comprehensive, actionable strategy is a significant challenge. It involves thorough planning, careful consideration of various factors, and a commitment to ongoing learning and adaptation. This section provides a step-by-step guide to developing an effective AI strategy.

Defining Your AI Vision and Objectives

The first step in developing an AI strategy is defining your AI vision and objectives. This means clearly articulating what you hope to achieve with AI and how it aligns with your broader business goals. The objectives could range from improving customer service and enhancing operational efficiency to driving innovation and gaining a competitive edge. Your AI vision should be ambitious but also realistic, considering your current capabilities and resources.

Understanding Your AI Readiness

Once you have defined your AI vision and objectives, the next step is assessing your AI readiness. This involves evaluating your current capabilities, resources, and infrastructure to understand where you stand and what you need to achieve your AI objectives. Key areas to consider include your data readiness, technological infrastructure, talent and skills, organizational culture, and regulatory environment.

Identifying AI Opportunities and Use Cases

With a clear understanding of your AI readiness, you can then start identifying AI opportunities and use cases that align with your objectives. This involves understanding where AI can add value in your business processes, products, or services, and prioritizing these opportunities based on their potential impact and feasibility. It's crucial to involve stakeholders from across the organization in this process to ensure a holistic view of AI opportunities.

Developing AI Capabilities

Once you've identified your AI opportunities, the next step is developing the necessary capabilities to seize these opportunities. This may involve investing in new technologies or tools, upskilling or hiring new talent, and setting up processes for data management and analytics. It's also important to foster a culture of innovation and learning, encouraging experimentation and adaptation as you navigate your AI journey.

Implementing AI Initiatives

With your AI capabilities in place, you can then start implementing your AI initiatives. This involves developing and testing AI models, integrating them into your business processes, and monitoring their performance. It's crucial to adopt an iterative approach, continually learning from your successes and failures, and refining your models and strategies accordingly.

Managing Risks and Ethical Considerations

As part of your AI strategy, you should also have a plan for managing risks and ethical considerations. This includes setting up mechanisms for ensuring data privacy and security, monitoring for algorithmic bias, and addressing any ethical issues that arise. It's also important to stay abreast of regulatory developments in the AI field and ensure your AI initiatives are compliant.

Measuring AI Success

Lastly, you need to define metrics for measuring AI success. These metrics should be aligned with your AI objectives and provide insights into the impact of your AI initiatives. Regularly tracking these metrics will help you assess your progress, identify areas for improvement, and demonstrate the value of AI to stakeholders.

Developing an effective AI strategy is a complex, ongoing process that requires a deep understanding of your business, a clear vision for AI, and a commitment to learning and adaptation. While the path to AI success may not always be smooth, a well-planned and well-executed AI strategy can help you navigate this path effectively, unlocking the full potential of AI for your business.

Sustaining and Scaling AI Initiatives

The journey of AI doesn't stop at the successful implementation of AI projects. In fact, the real challenge lies in sustaining and scaling these initiatives across the organization. To truly gain the benefits of AI, businesses must aim to scale beyond isolated use cases or experiments.

A successful AI strategy must consider how AI initiatives can be generalized and applied across different parts of the organization. It's important to build AI solutions that are not one-off, but repeatable and scalable. Businesses should aim to create an AI-infused environment where machine learning models and AI applications can be developed, deployed, and managed at scale.

Sustaining AI initiatives involves the continuous monitoring, maintenance, and improvement of AI systems. AI models need to be updated regularly to reflect new data, changing conditions, or shifts in business strategy. This is a significant task that often involves data scientists, IT teams, and business stakeholders.

Building an AI Culture

Last, but by no means least, an effective AI strategy must involve the cultivation of an AI culture. To fully leverage the potential of AI, organizations must foster a culture that values data-driven decision making, encourages experimentation and learning from failure, and promotes collaboration across different teams and functions.

This involves not only training employees in technical skills, but also promoting an understanding of AI and its potential benefits and challenges across the organization. It means encouraging a mindset of curiosity, adaptability, and continuous learning, which are essential for navigating the rapidly evolving AI landscape.

Regularly Revisiting Your AI Strategy

Given the fast-paced nature of AI, organizations must commit to regularly revisiting and updating their AI strategy. This means not only tracking progress against objectives and making necessary adjustments, but also staying abreast of new developments and trends in the AI field. It involves maintaining a forward-looking perspective and being willing to pivot your strategy as needed.

In conclusion, developing an effective AI strategy is a complex and ongoing process. It requires a clear vision, careful planning, and a commitment to continuous learning and adaptation. But with the right approach, it can unlock significant benefits for your business, from improved efficiency and effectiveness to increased innovation and competitiveness.

Chapter 8

AI and Data: Creating a Robust Data Infrastructure

A

rtificial Intelligence (AI) has been likened to the electricity of the 21st century because of its profound potential to revolutionize industries and transform business operations. However, AI's power doesn't come from vacuum; it thrives on data. Data is the lifeblood of AI, the raw material that fuels its algorithms and drives its insights. Without a robust data infrastructure, an organization's AI initiatives are likely to falter.

In this chapter, we delve into the critical relationship between AI and data, focusing on the importance of creating a robust data infrastructure to support your AI initiatives. We begin by exploring why a strong data infrastructure is necessary for AI and how it underpins successful AI implementation. We will provide you with a clear understanding of the different components of a data infrastructure and how they work together to support AI.

Next, we will discuss the challenges that organizations often face when building a data infrastructure for AI, from data quality issues to privacy concerns, and provide guidance on how to overcome these challenges. We will also delve into the importance of data governance and how to establish effective data governance practices.

Moreover, we will examine case studies of organizations that have successfully built robust data infrastructures to support their AI initiatives, providing practical insights and lessons learned.

Finally, we will look towards the future, discussing emerging trends in data and AI, and their implications for data infrastructure.

Whether you are just starting your AI journey or looking to scale your AI initiatives, this chapter will provide you with the knowledge and insights you need to build a robust data infrastructure that powers your AI strategy.

The Importance of Data in AI

The value of Artificial Intelligence (AI) in the business world is now widely acknowledged. However, the role of data as the fundamental building block of AI is often overlooked. Data is the key input for AI algorithms, providing the information they need to learn, make predictions, and generate insights. In this section, we explore why data is so important in AI, and how a robust data infrastructure underpins successful AI initiatives.

Data as the Fuel for AI

AI algorithms, particularly those based on machine learning, learn from data. They analyze the input data, identify patterns and relationships, and use these to make predictions or decisions. The quality and quantity of data directly influence the accuracy and reliability of AI predictions. The more high-quality data an AI system has access to, the better it can learn and the more accurate its outputs will be. Therefore, data can be seen as the fuel that powers AI. Without sufficient data, AI algorithms cannot function effectively.

Data Diversity for Comprehensive Learning

The diversity of data is equally important for AI. A well-rounded AI system needs a diverse dataset that covers different scenarios, conditions, and variables. This ensures that the AI algorithm can learn from a wide range of situations and can generalize its learnings to new, unseen data. If the dataset lacks diversity, the AI system may fail to perform well in real-world conditions, a problem known as overfitting.

Data Quality for Reliable AI Outputs

The quality of data is crucial for AI. AI systems require clean, accurate, and consistent data to function correctly. Poor quality data can lead to inaccurate predictions and unreliable outputs, undermining the value of AI. Therefore, data cleaning and preprocessing are vital steps in any AI project.

Data for Continuous Learning and Improvement

AI systems are not static; they need to continuously learn and adapt to changing conditions. This requires a steady stream of fresh data. By constantly updating the AI system with new data, organizations can ensure that their AI models remain accurate and relevant, improving their performance over time.

Data for Explainability and Trust

Data plays a vital role in enhancing the explainability and trustworthiness of AI systems. By providing transparent and interpretable data, organizations can help users understand how AI systems make decisions, increasing their trust in AI. Data can also be used to audit and verify the performance of AI systems, ensuring they behave as expected.

Data Infrastructure: The Foundation of AI

A robust data infrastructure is the foundation of any successful AI initiative. It provides the necessary tools and systems to collect, store, process, and analyze data at scale. A well-designed data infrastructure ensures that data is easily accessible, reliable, and secure, enabling organizations to fully leverage their data for AI.

In conclusion, data is the lifeblood of AI. It provides the raw material that AI algorithms need to learn and make predictions. A robust data infrastructure enables organizations to collect, process, and analyze data efficiently and effectively, maximizing the value of their AI initiatives. Understanding the importance of data in AI is the first step towards building a successful AI strategy.

Building a Data-Driven Culture

Understanding and acknowledging the importance of data is crucial, but it's equally important to build a data-driven culture within the organization. This means encouraging everyone within the business, not just the data scientists and AI specialists, to use data in their decision-making processes. When data is incorporated into the fabric of the organization, it becomes easier to collect, manage, and use effectively.

Data Ethics and Privacy

As we rely more on data, ethical considerations become increasingly important. Companies must ensure they are collecting and using data in a way that respects privacy and complies with data protection regulations. This includes obtaining proper consent for data collection, anonymizing data to protect individuals' identities, and being transparent about how data is used.

Data for Measuring AI Performance

Data is not only used to power AI algorithms but also to measure their performance. Without data, it's impossible to know whether an AI system is meeting its objectives. Key performance indicators (KPIs) should be established, and data should be collected and analyzed regularly to assess the effectiveness of AI initiatives.

The Role of Big Data in AI

The advent of big data – vast quantities of data generated at high velocity – has been a game-changer for AI. Big data allows for more complex modeling and more accurate predictions, and it opens new possibilities for AI, from real-time decision making to advanced personalization. However, managing and processing big data requires advanced data infrastructure, including high-performance storage systems and powerful data processing tools.

Conclusion

The importance of data in AI cannot be overstated. Data is the raw material that fuels AI, and a robust data infrastructure is essential for any successful AI initiative. By understanding the role of data in AI, businesses can better plan their AI strategies and invest in the right data infrastructure. In the next sections, we will delve deeper into the different components of a data infrastructure and how to build one that supports your AI initiatives.

Building a Robust Data Infrastructure

A robust data infrastructure is integral to leveraging the full potential of AI in business. It involves creating an ecosystem where data can be collected, stored, processed, and accessed effectively and securely. In this section, we will delve into the components of a robust data infrastructure and provide insights into building one for your business.

The Components of a Data Infrastructure

A data infrastructure consists of several key components:

Data Collection: This involves gathering data from various sources. Data can be structured (like numbers, dates, and groups of words called strings), unstructured (like text, images, and social media posts), or semi-structured (like XML or JSON files).

Data Storage: This involves storing the data securely and in a manner that can be accessed easily. Modern businesses use databases, data warehouses, or data lakes depending on their needs.

Data Processing: This involves cleaning, transforming, and preparing data for analysis. Data processing ensures that the data is accurate, complete, and in a format that can be utilized by AI algorithms.

Data Analysis: This involves analyzing the processed data to extract meaningful insights. This step is where AI comes into play – AI algorithms can analyze massive amounts of data much faster and more accurately than humans can.

Data Security: This involves ensuring that the data is protected from unauthorized access, corruption, or theft. Data privacy regulations like GDPR also require businesses to protect their data.

Key Considerations for Building a Data Infrastructure

When building a data infrastructure, consider the following:

Scalability: The data infrastructure should be able to handle increasing amounts of data as your business grows.

Flexibility: The infrastructure should be able to handle different types of data (structured, unstructured, and semi-structured) and support different types of analysis.

Security: The infrastructure should have strong security measures in place to protect the data.

Compliance: The infrastructure should enable your business to comply with relevant data privacy regulations.

Building a Data Infrastructure for AI

Building a data infrastructure for AI involves additional considerations. AI algorithms require massive amounts of high-quality data, so the data infrastructure must be designed to support this.

Data Storage for AI: AI applications typically require a data lake rather than a traditional data warehouse. This is because data lakes can store vast amounts of raw data in its original format, which gives AI algorithms more to work with.

Data Processing for AI: AI applications also require advanced data processing capabilities. This includes the ability to clean and preprocess data, handle missing or unbalanced data, and perform feature extraction.

Real-Time Data for AI: Many AI applications require real-time data processing and analysis. The data infrastructure should be able to support this.

Leveraging Cloud-Based Data Infrastructure

Cloud-based data infrastructure solutions can provide the scalability, flexibility, and advanced capabilities needed for AI. They can also provide cost savings, as businesses only pay for the storage and computing power they use.

Conclusion

Building a robust data infrastructure is a complex task that requires careful planning and execution. However, the rewards can be significant, as a well-designed data infrastructure is key to unlocking the full potential of AI. By considering the needs of your AI applications and leveraging advanced solutions like cloud-based data infrastructure, you can build a data infrastructure that supports your AI initiatives and drives your business forward.

Chapter 9

Building an AI-Ready Organization

T

he surge in technological advancements has brought Artificial Intelligence (AI) to the forefront of business transformation. AI isn't just a novelty anymore, it's a crucial component that can drive a competitive edge, influence decision-making, and shape the future of an organization. However, integrating AI is not a mere technological shift; it demands a broader organizational readiness.

In this chapter, we will discuss how to build an AI-ready organization. We'll explore the necessary steps to prepare your business for AI integration, the cultural shifts required, strategies to manage change, and the importance of developing an AI-skilled workforce. The goal is to offer a comprehensive guide on transforming your organization into a forward-thinking, AI-ready entity that is prepared to harness the power of this transformative technology.

By the end of this chapter, you'll have a clear understanding of the essential elements of an AI-ready organization and practical strategies to cultivate an environment conducive to AI adoption. Whether you're a startup seeking to build your business on an AI foundation, or an established company looking to infuse AI into your existing processes, this chapter will provide you with valuable insights to embark on your AI journey.

Cultivating AI Skills and Talent

Artificial Intelligence is a transformative technology, but it is only as good as the people who use and manage it. The success of AI within an organization largely depends on the skills and talents of its workforce. Therefore, cultivating AI skills and talent is a critical step in creating an AI-ready organization. This involves hiring the right people, training existing staff, fostering a culture of learning, and creating an organizational structure that supports AI.

Hiring the Right People

The first step in cultivating AI skills is to hire individuals with the necessary expertise. This could include data scientists, AI specialists, machine learning engineers, and other roles specific to your AI needs. However, hiring for AI roles can be challenging given the high demand and short supply of these skills in the job market. Therefore, organizations may need to look beyond traditional hiring methods. This could involve partnerships with universities, participation in AI competitions, or even the use of AI itself to identify potential candidates.

Training Existing Staff

In addition to hiring new talent, organizations must also focus on training existing staff. This involves identifying the AI skills that are most relevant to your business and providing employees with the resources and opportunities to acquire these skills. Training could take the form of online courses, workshops, or on-the-job training. The goal is not to turn every employee into an AI expert, but rather to create a workforce that understands the basics of AI and can work effectively with AI technologies.

Fostering a Culture of Learning

Building an AI-ready organization requires more than just skills – it requires a culture that values learning and innovation. This is because AI is a rapidly evolving field, and what is cutting-edge today may be obsolete tomorrow. Therefore, organizations must create an environment where continuous learning is encouraged and rewarded. This could involve promoting a growth mindset, providing time and resources for learning, and recognizing employees who take the initiative to improve their AI skills.

Creating an Organizational Structure that Supports AI

Finally, organizations must create an organizational structure that supports AI. This involves breaking down silos and encouraging collaboration between different departments. AI initiatives often require a cross-functional team that includes not only AI specialists, but also business analysts, IT professionals, and others who understand the organization's strategic objectives. Therefore, organizations must create a structure that facilitates communication and cooperation across these different roles.

The Role of Leadership

Leadership plays a critical role in cultivating AI skills and talent. Leaders must set the vision for AI within the organization, allocate resources for AI initiatives, and lead by example in terms of learning and adopting AI. They must also manage the change that comes with AI, addressing fears and resistance, and steering the organization through the transition period.

Conclusion

Cultivating AI skills and talent is a complex, ongoing process that requires a strategic and comprehensive approach. However, the rewards can be significant. By investing in the right people, training, and culture, organizations can create a workforce that is not only ready for AI, but also capable of leveraging it to drive innovation and growth. Building an AI-ready organization is not just about technology – it's about people. And with the right skills and talent, any organization can harness the power of AI.

Fostering an AI-Ready Culture

As organizations prepare for the integration of Artificial Intelligence (AI), one of the most significant challenges lies not in the technology itself but in the human aspect – fostering a culture that is ready to embrace AI. Building an AI-ready culture means instilling a mindset that welcomes innovation, encourages experimentation, values data, and is ready to adapt to the changes that AI brings.

Understanding the Importance of Culture

Organizational culture is a set of shared beliefs, values, practices, and assumptions that guide how an organization operates. It influences everything from decision-making processes to the way employees interact. When it comes to AI, the organizational culture can determine how quickly and effectively AI is adopted.

Instilling a Mindset of Innovation and Experimentation

AI is a rapidly evolving field, which means that organizations need to be open to change and willing to innovate. This requires a mindset that encourages experimentation and is not afraid to fail. Organizations can foster this mindset by encouraging employees to think outside the box, providing them with the resources they need to experiment with new ideas, and celebrating both successes and constructive failures.

Valuing Data

At the heart of AI is data. To effectively implement AI, organizations need to value data and understand its importance in decision making. This means creating a culture where data is respected, properly managed, and used responsibly. It also means training employees to understand data and use it effectively.

Preparing for Change

Adopting AI often means significant changes in the way an organization operates. Preparing for this change is a crucial part of building an AI-ready culture. This may involve managing employee expectations, providing training and support, and leading change management efforts.

The Role of Leadership

Leadership plays a critical role in fostering an AI-ready culture. Leaders set the tone for the organization, and their attitudes towards AI can greatly influence the rest of the staff. Leaders need to show enthusiasm for AI, demonstrate its potential value, and lead by example in embracing change.

Overcoming Resistance

Resistance to change is a common obstacle in implementing AI. Overcoming this resistance requires clear communication about the benefits of AI, addressing employee concerns, and involving employees in the AI implementation process. It also requires patience, as changing an organizational culture is a gradual process.

Building Trust in AI

For employees to embrace AI, they need to trust it. Building this trust involves demonstrating the reliability of AI systems, being transparent about how they work, and showing how they can help employees in their work.

Conclusion

Fostering an AI-ready culture is a challenging but vital part of preparing for AI. It requires a commitment to change, a willingness to innovate, and strong leadership. However, the rewards can be significant. An organization with an AI-ready culture is better prepared to harness the power of AI, adapt to its changes, and capitalize on its benefits. The future belongs to those who are ready for AI, and building an AI-ready culture is a key step in that direction.

Chapter 10

Ensuring Responsible AI Use in Business

I

n this chapter, we venture into the realm of responsibility and ethics as they pertain to AI use in business. Artificial Intelligence has ushered in a new era of technology, creating opportunities and challenges alike. While it has streamlined operations, automated mundane tasks, and opened avenues for innovative solutions, it has also given rise to new ethical dilemmas and questions of responsibility.

AI systems, by their very nature, have the potential to influence business decisions, customer relationships, and even societal norms. Therefore, it becomes imperative for businesses to ensure responsible AI use. This involves creating guidelines for ethical AI practices, understanding the potential risks and implications, and establishing strong governance structures to oversee AI use.

In this chapter, we'll discuss the importance of responsible AI use in business, explore the ethical considerations that need to be considered, and provide guidance on how businesses can ensure they're using AI in a responsible and ethical manner.

Ethical Considerations for AI

Artificial Intelligence (AI) has significantly transformed businesses across multiple sectors. However, as AI becomes more prevalent, the ethical considerations surrounding its use have also become increasingly important. Ethical considerations guide how businesses should responsibly deploy AI technology while maintaining respect for human rights and dignity.

Understanding AI Ethics

AI ethics concern the moral issues raised by the deployment of AI in society. They deal with questions like: Who is responsible when an AI makes a mistake? How do we ensure that AI systems are fair and do not perpetuate biases? How do we protect privacy when AI systems are trained on vast amounts of personal data? How do we ensure transparency in AI decision-making processes?

Fairness and Bias in AI

One of the significant ethical considerations for AI is ensuring fairness and avoiding bias. AI systems are trained on data, and if that data contains biases, the AI system can perpetuate and even amplify those biases. Businesses need to be cautious about the data they use to train their AI systems and implement methods to detect and mitigate bias.

Privacy and Data Protection

AI systems often rely on large amounts of data, some of which can be very personal. This raises concerns about privacy and data protection. Businesses need to ensure that they are collecting and using data in a way that respects privacy and complies with data protection laws. They also need to take precautions to protect data from breaches.

Transparency and Explainability

AI systems can sometimes act as 'black boxes,' with their decision-making processes being difficult to understand. This lack of transparency and explainability can make it hard to determine why an AI system made a particular decision, which can lead to trust issues. Businesses need to strive for transparency in their use of AI and seek to make their AI systems as explainable as possible.

Accountability and Responsibility

When an AI system makes a decision, who is responsible? This question of accountability and responsibility is a critical ethical consideration. Businesses need to have clear guidelines about who is responsible for the decisions made by their AI systems, especially when those decisions have significant impacts.

Impact on Jobs and Skills

AI has the potential to automate many tasks, leading to concerns about job displacement and changing skill requirements. Businesses need to consider the impact of their AI systems on jobs and ensure that they are supporting their employees through any transitions.

Conclusion

Ethical considerations for AI are vast and complex. Businesses must navigate these considerations carefully to responsibly deploy AI technology. By doing so, they can reap the benefits of AI while also upholding their ethical obligations. As AI continues to evolve, so will the ethical landscape, and businesses must be prepared to continuously evaluate and adjust their AI ethics policies.

Regulation and Compliance in AI

Regulation and compliance in AI are rapidly evolving areas, with new laws and guidelines being established as technology continues to advance. This section delves into the importance of regulation and compliance, the current regulatory landscape, and how businesses can ensure they're adhering to these guidelines.

The Importance of Regulation and Compliance

As AI technologies become more advanced and more widely used, they're also becoming more influential. As such, they have the potential to cause harm if not properly regulated. Regulations are necessary to ensure that AI is used responsibly and ethically, and to prevent or mitigate any harmful effects.

Moreover, compliance with these regulations is crucial. Not only can non-compliance lead to legal penalties, but it can also damage a business's reputation and undermine trust among customers and stakeholders.

Current Regulatory Landscape

The current regulatory landscape for artificial intelligence (AI) is a complex mix of various national and international laws, regulations, and guidelines. For instance, within the European Union, the General Data Protection Regulation (GDPR) plays a significant role in AI regulation, particularly in terms of data protection and privacy.

In the United States, there is no overarching federal regulation specifically for AI. However, individual states have begun to enact their own laws. On a global scale, organizations such as the Organization for Economic Co-operation and Development (OECD) and the United Nations have established guidelines or principles for AI.

Ensuring Compliance

Compliance with AI regulations can be a daunting task due to the intricate nature of the technology and the ever-changing regulatory environment. However, there are several strategies businesses can adopt.

Firstly, businesses should stay abreast of the latest regulatory developments in their industry and jurisdiction. This could involve hiring a legal counsel or a compliance officer who specializes in AI.

Secondly, businesses should perform regular audits of their AI systems to detect any potential compliance issues. These audits should be thorough, examining all aspects of the AI system, from the data it's trained on to its decision-making processes.

Thirdly, businesses should establish strong data governance policies. This includes ensuring that data is collected and used in compliance with privacy regulations, and that adequate security measures are in place to safeguard data from breaches.

Regulatory Challenges and Considerations

There are several challenges and considerations associated with AI regulation and compliance. One of the key challenges is the rapid pace of technological change, which can make it difficult for regulations to stay current. Another challenge is the global nature of AI, which brings up issues about jurisdiction and enforcement.

Furthermore, while regulation is necessary to ensure ethical and safe use of AI, there's also a risk of over-regulation, which could potentially hinder innovation. Striking a balance between the need for regulation and the desire to promote innovation is a delicate task.

Conclusion

Regulation and compliance in AI are not just about adhering to the law; they're also about building trust. By demonstrating their commitment to responsible AI use, businesses can build trust with customers, stakeholders, and the wider public. As the regulatory landscape for AI continues to evolve, businesses must be prepared to adapt and to take a proactive approach to compliance.

Chapter 11

Leveraging AI for Business Growth

I

n Chapter 11, we shift our focus to the enormous potential of AI for propelling business growth. Organizations across the globe are harnessing the power of AI to streamline operations, enhance customer experience, innovate products and services, and uncover new business opportunities. The transformational impact of AI is not merely limited to big tech companies. Businesses of all sizes and across various sectors can reap the benefits of AI, provided they know how to leverage it effectively.

This chapter is designed to equip you with the knowledge and insights required to harness AI for your business growth. We will explore how AI can fuel various aspects of business growth, including efficiency, innovation, customer engagement, and strategic decision making.

In this journey, we will also address potential challenges and provide strategies to overcome them. Case studies and real-world examples will be shared to illustrate the tangible benefits of AI and inspire you to think about how you might apply these lessons to your own business context.

From understanding the importance of AI-driven growth strategies to exploring specific applications of AI in various business contexts, this chapter serves as your comprehensive guide to leveraging AI for business growth. So, let's commence this exciting journey into the world of AI-driven growth.

Opportunities for Growth with AI

Artificial Intelligence (AI) is not merely a set of sophisticated tools or advanced technologies; it's a game-changer, a catalyst that has the potential to redefine business landscapes and drive unprecedented growth. AI's transformative power lies in its ability to process vast amounts of data, learn from it, and make informed decisions or predictions – all at a speed and scale beyond human capabilities.

In this section, we'll explore various avenues where AI can open opportunities for business growth.

Efficiency and Productivity

First and foremost, AI offers the potential to dramatically improve efficiency and productivity. Whether it's automating routine tasks, reducing errors, or speeding up processes, AI can bring about significant time and cost savings. For example, Robotic Process Automation (RPA) can automate repetitive tasks like data entry, freeing up employees to focus on more strategic work. Similarly, AI-powered predictive maintenance can detect machine failures before they occur, reducing downtime and maintenance costs.

Customer Experience

AI can also greatly enhance the customer experience, a critical aspect of business growth. With AI, businesses can provide personalized experiences, recommend products, and offer support round the clock. Chatbots, for instance, can handle customer queries 24/7, delivering instant and accurate responses. AI's ability to analyze customer data can also be used to predict customer behavior and personalize offerings, leading to increased customer satisfaction and loyalty.

Innovation

AI is a powerful tool for innovation. With AI, businesses can develop new products, services, or business models that were not possible before. For example, AI can be used to analyze market trends and customer preferences, providing valuable insights for product development. Businesses can also use AI to offer personalized products or services, creating new revenue streams.

Data-Driven Decision Making

One of the most significant advantages of AI is its ability to turn data into actionable insights. With AI, businesses can analyze vast amounts of data in real-time, helping them make informed decisions. Whether it's identifying market trends, predicting customer behavior, or optimizing operations, AI can provide valuable insights that drive strategic decision-making.

Risk Mitigation

AI can also help businesses mitigate risks. For instance, AI can analyze patterns in financial transactions to detect fraudulent activities. It can also help in regulatory compliance by monitoring business operations and flagging potential violations.

Access to New Markets

AI can also open new markets for businesses. By analyzing market data, AI can help businesses identify untapped markets or customer segments. Additionally, AI-powered translation services can break down language barriers, allowing businesses to reach global audiences.

While these are just a few examples, the potential applications of AI for business growth are virtually limitless. However, it's essential to remember that successful AI implementation requires a clear understanding of your business objectives, the right talent and skills, and a robust data infrastructure.

As we move forward, we will delve deeper into each of these opportunities, providing you with a comprehensive understanding of how you can leverage AI for your business growth. We will also look at real-world examples of businesses that have successfully harnessed the power of AI, providing you with inspiration and practical insights.

Case Studies: AI and Business Growth

Artificial Intelligence has ushered in a wave of transformation across industries, spurring growth and delivering a competitive edge to businesses that have embraced it. Let's delve into some real-world case studies to understand how AI is shaping business growth.

Case Study 1: Netflix and Personalized Recommendations

Netflix, the streaming giant, has built its success on a foundation of AI and Machine Learning (ML). The company's AI-powered recommendation engine accounts for about 80% of the TV shows discovered by its users. By analyzing users' viewing habits, ratings, and preferences, the AI algorithm suggests tailored content for each user, thereby enhancing customer experience and increasing viewer engagement. This personalization has led to customer loyalty, reduced churn, and ultimately, growth in subscriber base and revenues.

Case Study 2: Amazon and Operational Efficiency

Amazon, a global leader in e-commerce, utilizes AI to improve operational efficiency and customer experience. One notable AI application is in its fulfillment centers where robots – powered by AI and ML – move around shelves of products, assisting human workers in picking and packing orders. This automation has significantly reduced the time taken to process an order, thereby increasing efficiency, cutting costs, and enabling faster deliveries. Amazon's AI-infused efficiency is a key contributor to its customer satisfaction and business growth.

Case Study 3: Starbucks and Predictive Analytics

Starbucks, the global coffeehouse chain, uses AI-powered predictive analytics for personalized marketing. Its digital flywheel, an AI-driven recommendation system, provides personalized offerings to customers based on their past orders, time of day, weather, and location. This has led to increased customer engagement, repeat purchases, and ultimately, growth in revenues. Starbucks also uses AI for inventory management, optimizing store layouts, and even creating new products, demonstrating how AI can spur innovation and growth.

Case Study 4: American Express and Fraud Detection

American Express leverages AI for fraud detection, a critical aspect of risk mitigation. It uses ML algorithms to analyze millions of transactions in real-time, detecting patterns and anomalies that could indicate fraudulent activities. This proactive approach has not only saved millions of dollars in potential fraud losses but also strengthened customer trust and loyalty, contributing to business growth.

Case Study 5: Salesforce and AI-Powered CRM

Salesforce, the leading CRM platform, uses its AI tool, Einstein, to provide predictive and prescriptive insights across sales, service, and marketing. Einstein's capabilities range from predicting sales opportunities and identifying trends to automating tasks and personalizing customer interactions. This has helped businesses using

Salesforce to enhance their efficiency, make data-driven decisions, and improve customer experiences, leading to increased sales and growth.

Case Study 6: Stitch Fix and AI-Driven Fashion

Stitch Fix, an online personal styling service, leverages AI to offer personalized fashion recommendations. It uses ML algorithms to analyze a multitude of data – from customers' size, style preferences, and feedback to fashion trends and item attributes. This allows the company to offer a highly personalized service, leading to satisfied customers, repeat business, and growth.

These case studies underscore how AI can drive business growth – whether through enhancing customer experiences, improving operational efficiency, spurring innovation, making data-driven decisions, or mitigating risks. However, the path to successful AI adoption isn't without its challenges, and requires a strategic approach, the right talent, and a robust data infrastructure. As we continue, we'll explore how businesses can navigate these challenges and build a successful AI strategy.

Chapter 12

The Future of AI in Business

A

s we turn the page to Chapter 12, we look beyond the present and into the realm of possibilities. The impact of AI on the business landscape has already been monumental, but what does the future hold? In this chapter, we will cast our eyes forward and explore the exciting and at times challenging road that lies ahead for AI in business.

The evolution of AI technology has been marked by tremendous leaps and bounds, causing transformative shifts in nearly every industry. From enhancing customer experiences to streamlining operations and driving innovation, AI's role in business is expanding and evolving at an unprecedented rate. Yet, we stand on the cusp of an era where AI's potential is far from fully realized.

In this chapter, we will delve into the anticipated trends in AI and examine their potential impact on business. We will explore how AI is set to redefine business practices, shape customer interactions, and disrupt traditional business models. We will also discuss the looming challenges and how businesses can navigate them effectively to leverage the power of AI.

The future of AI in business is a fascinating mix of opportunities and challenges, shaped by technological breakthroughs, regulatory dynamics, societal shifts, and strategic choices. As we journey through this chapter, we will unravel the myriad ways in which AI is poised to reshape the future of business.

So, let's venture forth into the uncharted territories of the future, filled with the promise of AI's transformative potential and its implications for businesses worldwide. Buckle up for an insightful journey into what lies ahead in the AI-driven world of business.

Predicting AI Trends

Predicting future trends is a complex exercise, especially when it comes to a rapidly evolving field like artificial intelligence. However, based on the current trajectory of AI development and adoption, we can make some educated assumptions about where we might be headed.

AI Democratization:

One of the most significant trends in the field of AI is democratization, making advanced AI technologies accessible to a broader range of people and organizations. The democratization of AI is largely driven by the development of user-friendly AI tools and platforms that do not require expert knowledge to use. This trend is expected to continue and expand, allowing businesses of all sizes and across all industries to harness the power of AI.

Explainable AI:

Explainability in AI, or the ability to understand and interpret AI decisions, is becoming increasingly important. As AI systems become more prevalent and influential, the demand for transparency and accountability grows. In the future, we can expect a greater emphasis on explainable AI, with models that not only make accurate predictions but also provide clear and understandable explanations for their decisions.

AI Ethics and Regulation:

As AI continues to permeate our lives and businesses, concerns about ethical implications and the need for regulation are escalating. Issues around privacy, bias, and control of AI systems are at the forefront of this discussion. We can anticipate an increased focus on developing ethical guidelines and regulatory frameworks for AI in the future.

Integration of AI and Other Emerging Technologies:

AI is not developing in isolation. It's evolving alongside other emerging technologies like blockchain, Internet of Things (IoT), and quantum computing. The integration of AI with these technologies holds immense potential for businesses, offering new ways to collect and analyze data, enhance security, and create innovative products and services.

Evolution of AI Capabilities:

AI's capabilities are continually evolving, with ongoing advancements in areas like natural language processing, computer vision, and machine learning. As these technologies mature, we can expect to see even more sophisticated AI applications in business, from highly personalized customer interactions to advanced predictive analytics.

Autonomous Systems:

Autonomous systems, from self-driving cars to drones and robots, are another key trend in AI. These systems are expected to become increasingly capable and prevalent in the future, transforming industries like transportation, logistics, and manufacturing.

Personalized AI:

With the growing capabilities of AI in data analysis and pattern recognition, personalized AI is becoming a reality. This trend will continue to grow, allowing businesses to offer highly personalized products, services, and experiences based on individual customer preferences and behaviors.

AI in Cybersecurity:

Cybersecurity is another area where AI is expected to play a significant role. As cyber threats become more sophisticated, AI and machine learning can help detect and respond to threats more quickly and accurately.

Predicting AI trends is by no means a precise science, given the speed at which the technology is evolving. However, by staying informed about the current trajectory and potential developments, businesses can prepare and position themselves to take full advantage of the transformative power of AI.

Preparing for the Future

As we look towards the future of AI in business, it becomes crucial for organizations to be proactive in preparing for this fast-approaching reality. Here are some strategies businesses can adopt to ready themselves for the AI-driven future:

Invest in AI Education and Training:

The first step in preparing for the future of AI is to invest in education and training. Employees at all levels, from executives to entry-level workers, should have a basic understanding of what AI is, how it works, and how it can be applied in a business context. More in-depth training may be necessary for those who will be directly involved in developing or working with AI systems.

Cultivate a Culture of Innovation and Adaptability:

AI represents a significant shift in how businesses operate, and it requires an equally significant shift in corporate culture. Businesses should foster a culture of innovation and adaptability, where new ideas are welcomed, experimentation is encouraged, and failure is seen as an opportunity to learn and grow.

Develop an AI Strategy:

Having a clear AI strategy is essential for navigating the future. This strategy should outline the company's AI goals, identify potential use cases for AI in the business, and detail the resources and investments that will be needed to achieve these goals. The strategy should also consider ethical and regulatory considerations and include plans for managing potential risks.

Build a Robust Data Infrastructure:

AI systems rely on data to function, so businesses will need a robust data infrastructure to support their AI initiatives. This involves not only the technical aspects of data storage and management but also the practices and policies for data governance and privacy.

Collaborate with AI Experts and Partners:

Given the complexity of AI, it can be beneficial to collaborate with experts and partners. This might involve hiring AI specialists, partnering with AI technology providers, or collaborating with research institutions. These collaborations can provide valuable expertise and resources to help businesses successfully implement and manage AI systems.

Experiment with AI Technologies:

One of the best ways to understand AI and its potential is to experiment with AI technologies. This could involve piloting AI projects, testing different AI platforms and tools, or participating in AI hackathons or challenges. Through experimentation, businesses can gain practical experience with AI and learn more about what it can and cannot do.

Monitor AI Trends and Developments:

The world of AI is constantly evolving, with new technologies, applications, and trends emerging all the time. Businesses should stay informed about these developments and consider how they might impact their industry and their AI strategy.

Consider the Ethical and Social Implications of AI:

As businesses prepare for the future of AI, they should also consider the ethical and social implications. This includes thinking about how AI might affect jobs and skills, how AI decisions can be made transparent and fair, and how personal data can be protected.

Prepare for AI Regulation:

While AI regulation is still in its early stages, it's likely to become a more significant factor in the future. Businesses should follow developments in AI regulation closely and be prepared to comply with any new laws or guidelines.

Foster a Long-Term Perspective:

AI is not just a passing trend—it's a transformative technology that's here to stay. As such, businesses should take a long-term perspective when planning their AI initiatives. This means thinking beyond immediate results and considering how AI can create sustained value for the business over time.

The future of AI in business holds immense potential, but it also presents new challenges and uncertainties. By proactively preparing for this future, businesses can position themselves to harness the power of AI and navigate the changes it brings with confidence and agility.

Chapter 13

Building an AI-Ready Organization

I

n the rapidly changing business landscape, artificial intelligence (AI) has emerged as a powerful driver of innovation, efficiency, and competitive advantage. However, reaping the full benefits of this transformative technology requires more than just adopting AI tools and solutions. It calls for building an AI-ready organization, one that is not only equipped with the necessary technological infrastructure, but also the right mindset, skills, and strategies to leverage AI effectively.

In this chapter, we delve into what it means to be an AI-ready organization. We explore the key components of an AI-ready organization, including a culture of learning and innovation, a workforce equipped with AI skills, a robust data infrastructure, and a strategic approach to AI adoption. We also examine the challenges that organizations often face in becoming AI-ready and offer practical strategies to overcome these obstacles.

Whether you are just starting your AI journey or looking to scale your AI initiatives, this chapter will provide valuable insights and guidance to help you transform your organization into one that is not only ready for AI, but capable of harnessing it to drive real business value. Join us as we delve into the critical process of building an AI-ready organization, preparing your enterprise for a future where AI is not just an advantage, but a necessity.

Developing an AI Strategy

In the contemporary business world, the development of an AI strategy is no longer a forward-thinking initiative; it's a critical necessity. As AI continues to permeate every facet of our lives, organizations that don't actively plan for AI integration are likely to be left behind.

AI strategy is a comprehensive plan outlining how an organization aims to leverage AI technologies to achieve its business objectives. It encapsulates everything from the choice of AI technologies to be adopted, the data infrastructure needed, the ethical considerations to be observed, and the specific business areas where AI will be deployed.

However, developing an AI strategy is not a straightforward task. It requires a deep understanding of both AI capabilities and the organization's business objectives, resources, and constraints. Here, we break down the process of developing an effective AI strategy into five key steps:

Understand AI Capabilities and Limitations

The first step in developing an AI strategy is understanding what AI can and cannot do. AI technologies, like machine learning, natural language processing, and computer vision, offer unprecedented opportunities for automation, efficiency, and insight generation. However, they also have limitations and can be resource intensive. Organizations need to familiarize themselves with the capabilities and constraints of different AI technologies to make informed decisions about their adoption.

Define Clear Business Objectives

AI is not a silver bullet that can solve all business problems. It is a tool that can help achieve specific business objectives more effectively.

Hence, the second step in developing an AI strategy is to define clear, measurable business objectives. These could range from improving customer service and operational efficiency to driving innovation and creating new revenue streams.

Assess Current Data Infrastructure

AI technologies are data-driven; they require high-quality, relevant data to function effectively. Therefore, an assessment of the organization's current data infrastructure is a critical step in developing an AI strategy. This involves examining the quality, quantity, and diversity of available data, the data management practices in place, and the organization's ability to gather and process data in real-time.

Identify AI Opportunities and Use Cases

Once the organization has a clear understanding of AI capabilities and its data infrastructure, it can start identifying potential AI opportunities and use cases that align with its business objectives. This could involve using AI to automate routine tasks, gain insights from data, personalize customer interactions, or create innovative products and services.

Plan for Implementation and Scaling

The final step in developing an AI strategy involves planning for implementation and scaling. This includes deciding on the AI technologies to be adopted, the necessary infrastructure upgrades, the teams and roles required, and the metrics for measuring success. It also involves planning for potential challenges, such as data privacy concerns, workforce resistance, and regulatory compliance issues.

Developing an AI strategy is not a one-off task, but an ongoing process that requires continuous learning, adaptation, and refinement as AI technologies evolve and business needs change. It is also a collaborative effort that involves input from different stakeholders, including business leaders, IT teams, data scientists, and even customers.

By following these steps, organizations can develop a robust AI strategy that not only helps them adopt AI technologies effectively but also leverages these technologies to drive significant business value. However, it is important to remember that a strategy, no matter how well-crafted, is only as good as its execution. Therefore, organizations also need to focus on effective execution of their AI strategy, which involves fostering an AI-ready culture, upskilling the workforce, and ensuring responsible and ethical AI use.

Building a Data Infrastructure

In an era where data is considered the new oil, building a robust data infrastructure is imperative for any organization seeking to leverage AI technologies effectively. AI models, after all, are only as good as the data that feeds them. By investing in a robust data infrastructure, organizations can ensure that their AI technologies have the necessary resources to deliver valuable insights and drive meaningful business outcomes.

When we talk about data infrastructure, we refer to the technologies, processes, and policies that enable data collection, storage, management, and analysis. This involves everything from databases and data warehouses to data integration tools and data governance policies. Here, we delve into the process of building a robust data infrastructure, outlining the key steps and considerations involved.

Define Your Data Needs

The first step in building a data infrastructure is to define your data needs. This involves understanding what data you need, why you need it, and how you intend to use it. What types of data are relevant to your business objectives? What volume of data do you anticipate handling? What level of data quality is required? The answers to these questions will help guide your data infrastructure development efforts.

Choose the Right Data Storage and Management Solutions

Once you have a clear understanding of your data needs, the next step is to choose the right data storage and management solutions. This could involve on-premises databases, cloud-based data warehouses, or a hybrid solution. The choice will depend on a variety of factors, including your data volume, scalability needs, security requirements, and budget constraints.

Establish Data Integration Processes

Data integration is a critical aspect of data infrastructure. It involves consolidating data from various sources into a unified view, allowing for more effective analysis and decision-making. This could involve the use of data integration tools, data APIs, or data pipelines. The goal is to ensure that your data is easily accessible and usable for your AI technologies.

Implement Data Governance Policies

Data governance refers to the overall management of the availability, usability, integrity, and security of data used in an enterprise. This includes everything from data quality management and data privacy compliance to data lifecycle management. By implementing effective data governance policies, organizations can ensure that their data infrastructure is not just robust, but also compliant and trustworthy.

Plan for Scalability and Flexibility

As your organization grows and evolves, so will your data needs. Therefore, it is important to build a data infrastructure that is scalable and flexible. This means choosing solutions that can handle increasing data volumes and varying data types, as well as ones that can integrate with other technologies as your tech stack evolves.

Foster a Data-Driven Culture

Finally, building a robust data infrastructure is not just about the technology; it's also about the people and the culture. Organizations need to foster a data-driven culture where data is valued as a key asset, data literacy is promoted, and data-driven decision-making is the norm.

Building a robust data infrastructure is a complex, ongoing process. It requires significant investment in terms of time, money, and resources. However, the payoffs can be substantial. With a robust data infrastructure, organizations can ensure that their AI technologies are set up for success, equipped with the data they need to generate valuable insights and drive meaningful business outcomes. In this sense, data infrastructure serves as the foundation for effective AI adoption and use.

Cultivating an AI-Ready Culture

Once the data infrastructure is in place, the next key step in building an AI-ready organization is to implement AI capabilities. This involves developing or adopting AI algorithms, integrating them into business processes, and creating systems for their ongoing management and improvement.

Identify Opportunities for AI

The first step in implementing AI is to identify where it can have the most impact on your organization. This might involve automating repetitive tasks, improving decision-making with predictive analytics, enhancing customer engagement through personalized recommendations, or innovating business models with AI-driven services.

Develop or Adopt AI Algorithms

Once the opportunities have been identified, the next step is to develop or adopt the appropriate AI algorithms. This could involve building custom models with machine learning techniques, using pre-built AI services from cloud providers, or adopting open-source AI algorithms. The choice will depend on your data, the problem you are trying to solve, your technical capabilities, and your budget.

Integrate AI into Business Processes

Simply having AI algorithms is not enough; they need to be integrated into your business processes to deliver value. This might involve embedding AI into your customer service systems for automated responses, integrating AI into your supply chain for demand forecasting, or using AI in your HR processes for talent acquisition and management.

Create Systems for Ongoing Management and

Improvement

AI is not a one-and-done deal. For AI to deliver sustained value, there need to be systems in place for its ongoing management and improvement. This might involve monitoring the performance of your AI models, retraining them with new data, or fine-tuning them to improve their accuracy.

Ensure Ethical and Responsible AI Use

Finally, it is crucial to ensure that AI is used ethically and responsibly in your organization. This involves understanding the potential biases in your AI algorithms, being transparent about AI use with your stakeholders, and being prepared to explain AI decisions when necessary.

In summary, implementing AI capabilities in an organization involves identifying the right opportunities, developing or adopting the right AI algorithms, integrating them into business processes, and creating systems for their ongoing management and improvement. While this process can be complex, the potential benefits - in terms of increased efficiency, improved decision-making, enhanced customer engagement, and business model innovation - make it a worthwhile investment. By carefully planning and executing your AI implementation, you can set your organization up for success in the AI era.

Chapter 14
Ensuring Responsible AI Use in Business

L

ooking further into the 21st century, the use of AI in business is no longer a mere novelty—it's a necessity for staying competitive. However, with the widespread adoption of AI come various ethical, legal, and social implications that businesses must address.

This chapter, "Ensuring Responsible AI Use in Business," takes a deep dive into the responsible usage of AI in the corporate world. It emphasizes the importance of ethically sound AI practices, explores the regulatory landscape surrounding AI, and suggests practical ways organizations can ensure accountability and transparency in their AI endeavors.

We will discuss how to mitigate the risk of bias in AI, protect data privacy, and maintain security in AI systems. We will also examine the role of governments and international bodies in shaping AI regulations, and how businesses can comply with these laws while leveraging the power of AI.

In an era where technology often outpaces regulation, it is crucial for organizations to proactively address these issues—not just to avoid potential legal ramifications, but also to build trust with their customers and stakeholders, and to contribute to a fair and just digital society.

This chapter is essential reading for anyone who wants to understand the complex terrain of responsible AI use in business. The insights offered here will equip you with the knowledge and foresight to navigate the ethical challenges of AI, ensuring that your business not only stays competitive, but also operates with integrity in the age of AI.

Ethical AI

In our current digital age, the realm of artificial intelligence (AI) has become increasingly pervasive in our daily lives. As such, the ethical implications of AI systems have risen to the forefront of public consciousness. The ethical use of AI is no longer an abstract concept debated in academic circles, but a tangible concern that impacts every individual and organization. It is, therefore, essential to explore and understand the concept of ethical AI.

Ethical AI refers to the practice of designing, developing, and deploying AI systems in a manner that respects human rights and values, ensures fairness, maintains transparency, and promotes overall wellbeing. It requires an alignment of AI systems and applications with the principles of ethical conduct, emphasizing respect for the dignity, rights, and freedoms of all individuals.

One of the most critical aspects of ethical AI is the prevention of bias. AI systems, like all technologies, are not inherently neutral. They can reflect and even amplify the biases of their creators, or the biases present in the data used to train them. This can lead to discrimination and unfair treatment, often impacting the most vulnerable populations. For example, an AI hiring system trained on data from a company with a history of gender discrimination may inadvertently continue that discrimination, screening out qualified female candidates in favor of male ones. Ensuring that AI systems are free of bias is not just an ethical necessity, but also a business imperative, as biased AI can lead to bad decisions, reputational damage, and legal liabilities.

In addition to preventing bias, ethical AI also involves protecting privacy and security. AI systems often require vast amounts of data to function effectively, and this data frequently involves sensitive personal information. Businesses must ensure that their AI systems respect individuals' privacy rights and comply with data protection laws. This involves not just securing data against breaches, but also being transparent about how data is collected, stored, and used, and giving individuals control over their data.

Furthermore, ethical AI requires transparency and explainability. As AI systems become more complex, it can be challenging to understand how they make decisions. This lack of transparency, often referred to as the "black box" problem, can lead to mistrust and accountability issues. Businesses must strive to make their AI systems as transparent and explainable as possible, ensuring that stakeholders understand how decisions are made and that there is accountability when things go wrong.

Finally, ethical AI involves considering the broader social implications of AI. This includes the potential impact on employment, as AI automates certain jobs, and the digital divide, as those without access to AI technology get left behind. Businesses must consider these implications and strive to use AI in a way that benefits society.

In conclusion, ethical AI is a complex but crucial aspect of using AI in business. It involves navigating various challenges, from preventing bias and protecting privacy, to ensuring transparency and considering the broader social implications. However, by committing to ethical AI, businesses can not only avoid potential pitfalls but also build trust with their stakeholders, achieve better results, and contribute to a more equitable and just digital society. As we move forward into an increasingly AI-driven world, ethical AI will be not just an option, but a necessity.

AI Regulation

As the impact of artificial intelligence (AI) grows across industries and societies, the need for clear and robust regulation becomes increasingly apparent. Regulation of AI is essential for establishing accountability, ensuring ethical use, protecting individual rights, and preserving societal values.

AI regulation refers to the laws, rules, and guidelines designed to govern the development, deployment, and use of AI technologies. These regulatory measures aim to manage the risks associated with AI, mitigate its potential harms, and maximize its benefits for society. They cover a wide range of areas, from data privacy and cybersecurity to algorithmic transparency, bias prevention, and much more.

One key area of AI regulation is data privacy. As AI systems often rely on vast amounts of data, including personal and sensitive information, they pose significant privacy risks. Regulatory measures, such as the European Union's General Data Protection Regulation (GDPR) or the California Consumer Privacy Act (CCPA) in the U.S., set rules for data collection, processing, storage, and sharing, ensuring that individuals' privacy rights are respected and that businesses handle data responsibly.

Another crucial aspect of AI regulation is algorithmic transparency and accountability. As AI systems become more complex, understanding how they make decisions – the so-called "black box" problem – becomes increasingly challenging. Regulations can require businesses to design their AI systems to be transparent and explainable, enabling stakeholders to understand how decisions are made and ensuring accountability when things go wrong.

AI regulation also encompasses fairness and non-discrimination. AI systems can inadvertently perpetuate or amplify biases present in their training data or algorithms, leading to unfair or discriminatory outcomes. Regulatory measures can mandate businesses to test their

AI systems for bias, implement measures to reduce bias, and take responsibility for any discriminatory effects.

Moreover, AI regulation can also address the societal implications of AI. This includes the potential impact on employment, as certain jobs become automated, and the digital divide, as those without access to AI technology get left behind. Governments can enact regulations to manage these impacts, such as retraining programs for workers displaced by AI or policies to ensure equitable access to AI technology.

However, the regulation of AI is not without its challenges. One challenge is the rapidly evolving nature of AI technology, which can make it difficult for regulations to keep up. Another challenge is the global nature of AI, which requires international cooperation to effectively regulate. Additionally, there is a need to balance regulation with innovation, as overly restrictive regulations could stifle the development of beneficial AI technologies.

Despite these challenges, the importance of AI regulation cannot be overstated. As AI continues to transform our world, the need for clear, robust, and forward-looking regulation grows. By regulating AI, we can ensure that it is used ethically and responsibly, that its benefits are maximized, and its potential harms are mitigated.

AI regulation is not just about managing risks, but also about shaping the future of AI in a way that aligns with our societal values and aspirations. It is about making sure that AI is used for the benefit of all, not just a few. It is about creating a future where AI is a tool for empowerment, not exploitation; for fairness, not discrimination; for openness, not opacity. And most importantly, it is about ensuring that in this future, we remain in control of AI, not the other way around.

In conclusion, AI regulation is a complex but crucial aspect of the AI landscape. It requires careful thought, broad consultation, and decisive action. It is not an easy task, but it is a necessary one. As we navigate the challenges and opportunities of the AI era, let us commit to a path of robust and responsible regulation - a path that leads to a future where AI serves humanity, respects our rights, and upholds our values.

Stakeholder Engagement in AI

In the rapidly advancing landscape of artificial intelligence (AI), stakeholder engagement is no longer a luxury but a necessity. It involves the active participation and collaboration of all parties who are impacted by or have an interest in the development, deployment, and governance of AI systems. These stakeholders range from internal entities like employees and managers to external parties like customers, investors, regulatory authorities, and the wider public.

Stakeholder engagement is a critical process for several reasons. Firstly, it brings diverse perspectives and insights into the decision-making process, enhancing the quality and credibility of decisions. Secondly, it ensures transparency and accountability, building trust among stakeholders. Lastly, it helps identify and address potential ethical, social, and legal issues related to AI, thus mitigating risks, and promoting responsible use of AI.

Internal stakeholders play a crucial role in the development and implementation of AI. Employees, for instance, can provide valuable insights into how AI can be used to improve operational efficiency, product quality, or customer service. They can also raise concerns about the potential impact of AI on their roles, job security, or workplace culture. By engaging employees, organizations can not only harness their insights but also address their concerns, ensuring a smoother transition to AI-enabled operations.

Managers and executives, on the other hand, are responsible for setting the strategic direction for AI in the organization. They need to understand the opportunities and challenges of AI, make informed decisions about AI investments, and lead the cultural and organizational changes required for successful AI adoption. Engaging these decision-makers can help align AI strategy with business strategy, promote leadership buy-in, and foster an AI-ready culture within the organization.

External stakeholders also have a crucial role to play. Customers, for instance, can provide feedback on how AI can enhance their experience, or express concerns about privacy, transparency, or fairness. By engaging customers, businesses can design AI solutions that truly meet customer needs, build customer trust, and enhance brand reputation.

Investors and shareholders, meanwhile, can influence the strategic direction of AI in the organization. They need to understand the financial implications of AI, assess the risks and returns of AI investments, and hold the organization accountable for its AI performance. Engaging these stakeholders can help secure financial support for AI initiatives, align AI strategy with shareholder expectations, and promote corporate accountability.

Regulatory authorities are another key stakeholder group. They set the rules for AI development and use, ensure compliance, and protect public interests. By engaging regulators, businesses can understand the legal requirements for AI, ensure compliance, and contribute to the shaping of AI policy.

Finally, the wider public - including civil society, academia, media, and the general population - also has a stake in AI. These stakeholders can raise awareness of societal issues related to AI, advocate for ethical and responsible AI, and hold businesses and governments accountable. Engaging the public can help ensure that AI serves societal interests, respects human rights, and is held to the highest ethical standards.

However, stakeholder engagement in AI is not without its challenges. These include identifying the relevant stakeholders, understanding their diverse interests and perspectives, facilitating meaningful participation, and managing conflicts of interest. Despite these challenges, the benefits of stakeholder engagement far outweigh the costs. It is a critical process for ensuring that AI is developed, deployed, and governed in a way that is ethical, responsible, and beneficial for all.

In conclusion, stakeholder engagement is a key component of responsible AI. It brings diverse voices to the table, fosters transparency and accountability, and helps ensure that AI serves the interests of all stakeholders. As we navigate the complex landscape of AI, let us commit to a path of inclusive and meaningful stakeholder engagement - a path that leads to a future where AI is not just about technology, but about people's values.

Chapter 15

Leading the AI Transformation

T

he AI revolution is upon us, changing the ways we work, live, and interact. AI's promise is significant, but its journey towards transformational impact isn't automatic or easy. It requires thoughtful and strategic leadership, a clear vision, and a commitment to navigate the complexities inherent in technological change. In this pivotal chapter, we will explore the qualities, strategies, and approaches necessary to effectively lead the AI transformation within an organization.

The successful adoption of AI isn't just about having the right technology; it is about having the right mindset and the right leadership. The leaders of tomorrow will need to be adaptive, agile, and open to learning. They will need to understand AI's potential, the ethical considerations it raises, and how to manage its impact on their teams and stakeholders.

In this chapter, we will delve into the complexities of leading an AI transformation. We will discuss the leadership traits and skills that are crucial in the age of AI, from strategic foresight and change management to ethical awareness and stakeholder engagement. We will also explore strategies for fostering an AI-ready culture, developing AI talent, and aligning AI with business strategy.

Leading the AI transformation is no small task, but with the right understanding, approach, and commitment, it is an undertaking that can yield unprecedented benefits. It is about more than just staying competitive; it is about shaping a future where AI is used responsibly and effectively to create value, improve lives, and solve the pressing challenges of our time. So, let's embark on this journey towards leading AI transformation.

Setting the AI Vision

Every transformative journey starts with a vision. A compelling, clear, and inspiring vision serves as the North Star guiding an organization towards its desired future state. In the context of AI transformation, the vision must articulate the strategic role of AI in the organization, the value it aims to create, and the principles that will govern its use. Let's explore how to craft such a vision and why it's a critical first step in leading AI transformation.

AI offers a broad array of applications, from process automation and predictive analytics to customer engagement and product innovation. But the broad possibilities of AI can also make it challenging for organizations to focus their efforts and resources. This is where a clear AI vision comes in. It helps the organization to concentrate its AI initiatives around the most strategic and value-adding opportunities. For example, a retail company might envision using AI to personalize customer experiences, while a manufacturing firm might focus on using AI to optimize its supply chain.

Setting the AI vision also involves anticipating the impacts of AI on the organization's people and processes. AI can bring significant changes in how work is performed, who performs it, and what skills are required. Leaders must articulate a vision that acknowledges these impacts and outlines the organization's commitment to managing them in a way that respects the interests of its employees, customers, and other stakeholders.

At the same time, the AI vision must not gloss over the challenges and ethical considerations of AI. It must express the organization's commitment to use AI responsibly, transparently, and in compliance with relevant laws and regulations. For instance, an organization might commit to using AI in a way that respects user privacy, avoids harmful bias, and promotes fairness and inclusivity.

Creating the AI vision is just the first step. The next challenge is to communicate it effectively throughout the organization. This involves articulating the vision in a way that is accessible, engaging, and meaningful to all members of the organization. Leaders must explain what the AI vision means for each team and individual and how it aligns with the organization's overall strategy and values.

It's also crucial to engage the organization in a dialogue around the AI vision. This can help to foster buy-in, generate ideas, and surface concerns or misconceptions about AI. It's a valuable opportunity for leaders to listen, learn, and demonstrate their commitment to a people-centric AI transformation.

Setting the AI vision is a continual process. As the organization learns from its AI initiatives and the AI landscape evolves, the vision might need to be refined. It's therefore essential for leaders to maintain an open mindset, embrace feedback, and stay informed about AI trends and best practices.

Lastly, the AI vision must be translated into actionable strategies and initiatives. This involves setting clear objectives, KPIs, and milestones that align with the AI vision. It also requires establishing governance structures and processes to oversee the execution of the AI strategy and ensure adherence to the AI principles outlined in the vision.

In conclusion, setting the AI vision is a critical leadership task in AI transformation. It requires a deep understanding of AI's potential and challenges, a clear strategic focus, and a commitment to ethical and people-centric AI use. With a compelling AI vision, leaders can inspire their organizations to embrace the AI journey and navigate it in a way that creates sustainable value and aligns with their core values and principles.

Fostering an AI-Ready Culture

Implementing an AI strategy requires more than technical know-how and state-of-the-art AI tools. It necessitates a cultural shift that permeates the entire organization. A culture that fosters curiosity, encourages innovation, prioritizes learning, and embraces change is more likely to successfully implement AI and reap its benefits. Creating an AI-ready culture is thus an essential step in any AI transformation journey.

An AI-ready culture begins with a shared understanding of AI. There should be a conscious effort to demystify AI, removing misconceptions and apprehensions surrounding it. This can be achieved through regular training and workshops tailored to different roles within the organization. The aim is not to turn everyone into a data scientist but to ensure everyone understands what AI can and cannot do, and how it can support their work.

Leaders play a crucial role in fostering an AI-ready culture. They must lead by example, embracing AI in their functions and demonstrating its utility. They should also show an openness to experimentation, acknowledging that the path to AI success includes inevitable failures and learning from them. This can help create a safe environment where employees feel encouraged to innovate and take calculated risks.

Encouraging cross-functional collaboration is also key to an AI-ready culture. AI initiatives often require the blending of skills from different areas such as data science, IT, business, and ethics. Breaking down silos can facilitate the exchange of ideas and perspectives, leading to more innovative and robust AI solutions.

Moreover, fostering an AI-ready culture involves creating a data-driven mindset. Data is the lifeblood of AI, and decisions should be based on data, not hunches or assumptions. This requires not only access to data but also the skills to interpret and use it effectively. Organizations should therefore invest in data literacy programs and promote data-driven decision-making at all levels.

In addition, ethical considerations should be ingrained into the culture. As AI systems often involve sensitive data and can significantly impact people's lives, ethical use of AI should be a core cultural value. This includes respect for privacy, fairness, transparency, and accountability. Ethical considerations should be incorporated into AI training programs and decision-making processes.

Lastly, an AI-ready culture requires a commitment to continuous learning. The field of AI is evolving rapidly, and staying abreast of the latest developments is crucial. Organizations should thus foster a learning culture, providing opportunities for employees to upskill and reskill. This could involve partnering with educational institutions, offering online learning resources, or providing time off for self-directed learning.

In conclusion, fostering an AI-ready culture is a multifaceted task. It requires efforts at all levels of the organization and touches upon various aspects such as knowledge of AI, leadership, collaboration, data-driven decision making, ethics, and continuous learning. It may be challenging, but the rewards are significant. An AI-ready culture can not only facilitate the successful implementation of AI but also contribute to a more innovative, agile, and resilient organization.

Ensuring Responsible AI Use

As organizations embark on their AI journey, they need to ensure that their use of AI is responsible and ethical. This involves addressing critical issues such as fairness, transparency, privacy, and accountability. Ensuring responsible AI use is not just about compliance with regulations; it's also about earning the trust of customers, employees, and other stakeholders.

A responsible AI framework starts with clear ethical guidelines. These guidelines should articulate the organization's commitment to using AI in a way that respects human rights, promotes fairness, and avoids harm. The guidelines should be specific enough to guide decision-making but flexible enough to adapt to new circumstances and technologies.

One of the key ethical issues in AI is bias. AI systems learn from data, and if the data is biased, the AI system can perpetuate or even exacerbate these biases. Therefore, organizations need to implement measures to identify and mitigate bias in their AI systems. This could involve diverse teams that can bring different perspectives, rigorous testing for bias, and transparency about how decisions are made.

Transparency is another crucial aspect of responsible AI use. Stakeholders should be able to understand how AI systems make decisions. This involves explainability, i.e., the ability to explain in human terms how the AI system arrived at a particular decision. However, transparency also extends to communication about the organization's AI strategy, policies, and practices. Openness about AI helps build trust and allows stakeholders to make informed decisions.

Privacy is a major concern in AI, as AI systems often rely on large amounts of personal data. Organizations must therefore ensure that their use of AI respects privacy rights. This involves not just compliance with data protection laws, but also ethical data practices such as data minimization, purpose limitation, and secure data storage and processing.

Accountability is a key component of responsible AI use. If something goes wrong with an AI system, it should be clear who is responsible. This requires clear lines of responsibility and robust oversight mechanisms. Moreover, organizations should have processes in place to rectify any harm caused by their AI systems.

Engaging stakeholders is another important aspect of responsible AI use. This involves not only communicating about AI but also listening to stakeholders' concerns and incorporating their input into decision-making. Stakeholder engagement can help identify potential issues early on, improve the acceptability of AI systems, and contribute to more equitable outcomes.

Finally, organizations need to build the necessary skills to ensure responsible AI use. This includes technical skills such as data science and AI ethics, but also soft skills such as critical thinking, ethical decision-making, and empathy. Training and development programs should therefore encompass a broad range of skills and be available to all employees, not just those directly involved in AI.

In conclusion, ensuring responsible AI use is a complex but crucial task. It requires a proactive and comprehensive approach, involving ethical guidelines, measures to address bias, transparency, privacy protection, accountability mechanisms, stakeholder engagement, and skills development. While challenging, responsible AI use can significantly enhance the benefits of AI and contribute to a more ethical and inclusive digital future.

Managing AI-Driven Change

The introduction of AI into any organization represents a significant change. This change isn't merely technical or operational, but also cultural and strategic. Managing this AI-driven change effectively requires a deep understanding of change management principles and a clear strategy for their application within the unique context of AI.

First and foremost, it is crucial to understand that AI is more than a set of technologies. It represents a new way of thinking and working. It demands a shift from a deterministic approach, where actions are pre-programmed, to a probabilistic approach, where decisions are made based on data and patterns. This shift can be challenging for many employees and requires significant change management efforts.

Managing AI-driven change involves several key components:

Creating a compelling vision: An effective AI strategy starts with a clear and compelling vision of how AI can support the organization's goals. This vision should be inspiring and compelling enough to motivate employees to embrace the change. It should also be clear and concrete enough to guide decision-making and action.

Communicating effectively: Communication is a critical element of change management. It is important to communicate the vision and strategy for AI clearly and consistently. Communication should also be two-way: organizations need to listen to employees' concerns and feedback and address them effectively.

Engaging stakeholders: Stakeholder engagement is crucial for the success of any change effort. This includes not only employees, but also customers, partners, regulators, and other stakeholders. Engaging stakeholders can help gain buy-in, identify potential obstacles, and develop solutions.

Building capabilities: AI requires new skills and capabilities, from data science to AI ethics. Organizations need to invest in training and development to build these capabilities. They also need to create an environment that encourages continuous learning and adaptation.

Managing resistance: Resistance is a natural part of any change process. Organizations need to anticipate resistance and manage it effectively. This involves understanding the sources of resistance, whether they are fear of change, lack of understanding, or concerns about job security, and addressing them directly and empathetically.

Piloting and scaling: It are often effective to start with small pilot projects to demonstrate the value of AI and learn from experience. Once the pilot projects have proven successful, they can be scaled up. Scaling AI requires careful planning and management to avoid common pitfalls such as data silos and algorithmic bias.

Monitoring and adjusting: Change is a process, not a one-time event. Organizations need to monitor the implementation of their AI strategy and adjust it as necessary. This involves not only tracking technical metrics such as model performance, but also organizational metrics such as employee engagement and customer satisfaction.

In conclusion, managing AI-driven change is a complex but crucial task. It requires clear vision, effective communication, stakeholder engagement, capability building, resistance management, careful piloting and scaling, and continuous monitoring and adjustment. With these elements in place, organizations can navigate the AI-driven change effectively and reap the full benefits of AI.

About the Author

Dan Pearson is a distinguished authority, innovator, and entrepreneur in the dynamic sphere of emerging technologies, with a professional tenure that spans over a decade. His career is a testament to his relentless pursuit of innovation and his dedication to exploring the untapped potential of technology.

Pearson's professional odyssey began in the cryptocurrency sector, where he utilized his expertise to guide novices into this groundbreaking financial domain. His trailblazing endeavors led to the creation of the successful platform, Bitcoin Investments, which was an indispensable guide for those venturing into the world of cryptocurrency.

Throughout his illustrious career, Pearson has consistently showcased a profound comprehension of technology's transformative power. His remarkable portfolio is replete with pioneering projects, including the unique Non-Fungible Token (NFT) series, Ninjoon, and the innovative Project Nexus.

Ninjoon, a distinctive NFT collection, consists of 1500 individual digital art pieces, each depicting a 'Ninjoon' with unique characteristics. This endeavor exemplifies Pearson's ability to leverage blockchain technology to foster value and engagement in the digital art realm.

Project Nexus, another revolutionary NFT initiative, harnesses the power of randomness and DALL-E Stable Diffusion to produce unique NFT artworks. This inventive project further cements Pearson's standing as a vanguard in the rapidly progressing NFT field.

Beyond his technological ventures, Pearson brings to the fore over a decade of managerial experience. His leadership acumen, coupled with his profound understanding of emerging technologies, uniquely positions him to steer businesses and individuals through the intricate landscape of AI and blockchain.

In his book, The AI Frontier: Unleashing the Power of Artificial Intelligence in Business," Pearson draws upon his vast knowledge and experience to guide readers through the transformative process of integrating AI into business. His astute insights and pragmatic advice make this book an indispensable guide for anyone aiming to comprehend and utilize the power of AI in the business world.

About the Author

Dan Pearson, a renowned innovator and entrepreneur, brings over a decade of expertise in emerging technologies. From cryptocurrencies to groundbreaking NFT projects like Ninjoon and Project Nexus, Pearson's deep understanding of technology's transformative potential is evident. In "The AI Frontier: Unleashing the Power of Artificial Intelligence in Business," he offers essential insights and practical guidance for integrating AI into the business landscape.

Read more at https://danpearson.net.